Re-evaluating residential care

RETHINKING AGEING SERIES

Series editor: Brian Gearing
School of Health and Social Welfare
The Open University

The rapid growth in ageing populations in Britain and other countries has led to a dramatic increase in academic and professional interest in the subject. Over the past decade this has led to the publication of many research studies which have stimulated new ideas and fresh approaches to understanding old age. At the same time, there has been concern about continued neglect of ageing and old age in the education and professional training of most workers in health and social services, and about inadequate dissemination of the new information and ideas about ageing to a wider public.

This series aims to fill a gap in the market for accessible, up-to-date studies of important issues in ageing. Each book will focus on a topic of current concern addressing two fundamental questions: what is known about this topic? And what are the policy, service and practice implications of our knowledge? Authors will be encouraged to develop their own ideas, drawing on case material, and their own research, professional or personal experience. The books will be interdisciplinary, and written in clear, non-technical language which will appeal to a broad range of students, academics and professionals with a common interest in ageing and age care.

Re-evaluating residential care

SHEILA PEACE
LEONIE KELLAHER
and
DIANNE WILLCOCKS

OPEN UNIVERSITY PRESS
Buckingham · Philadelphia

Open University Press
Celtic Court
22 Ballmoor
Buckingham
MK18 1XW

and
1900 Frost Road, Suite 101
Bristol, PA 19007, USA

First Published 1997

A catalogue record of this book is available from the British Library

ISBN 0 335 19392 7 (pbk)   0 335 19393 5 (hbk)

Library of Congress Cataloging-in-Publication Data

Peace, Sheila M.
  Re-evaluating residential care/Sheila Peace, Leonie Kellaher and Dianne
Willcocks
      p.   cm.— (Rethinking ageing series)
    Includes bibliographical references and index.
    ISBN 0-335-19393-5 (hc). — ISBN 0-335-19392-7 (pbk.)
    1. Aged — Institutional care — Evaluation. 2. Old age homes –
– Evaluation. 3. Nursing homes — Evaluation. I. Kellaher, Leonie, A.
    II. Willcocks, Dianne M. III. Title IV. Series.
HV1454.P43   1997
362.6' 1 — dc20   96-46517
                                                                      CIP

Typeset by Type Study, Scarborough
Printed in Great Britain by Biddles Limited, Guildford and Kings Lynn

To our parents:

Johanna and Reg
Thomas and Norah
Jack and Georgina

with love and fond memories

Contents

Series editor's preface

The rapid growth in ageing populations in this and other societies has led to a new academic and professional interest in gerontology. Since the mid-1970s, there has been a steady growth in research studies which have attempted to define the characteristics and needs of older people. Equally significant have been the very few theoretical attempts to reconceptualize what old age means and to explore new ways in which we may think about older people (among them Johnson 1976; Townsend 1981; Walker 1981). These two broad approaches which can be found in the literature on ageing – the descriptive (what do we know about older people?) and the theoretical (what do we understand about older people, and what does old age mean to them?) – can also be found in the very small number of post-graduate and professional training courses in gerontology which are principally intended for those who work with older people in the health and social services.

Concurrent with this growth in research-based knowledge, however, has been a growing concern about both the neglect of ageing and old age in the education and basic training of most workers in the health and social services, and the inadequate dissemination of new information and ideas to lay carers and a wider public. There is, in short, a gap between what we now comprehend about old age and the limited amount of knowledge and information which is readily available and accessible to professionals, voluntary workers and carers.

The main aim of the 'Rethinking Ageing' series has been to fill this gap with books which focus on a topic of current concern or interest in ageing. These topics have included, for example, health in old age; elder abuse; community care; race and ethnicity; and ageism. Each book addresses two fundamental questions. What is known about this topic? And what are the policy and practice implications of this knowledge?

The series has therefore focused on topics of current concern or interest to a primary audience who have a direct involvement in or concern with practice. However, all of the books published so far in the series have also attracted a significant further readership among researchers and postgraduate students who want a critical overview of an important contemporary topic in gerontology.

Re-evaluating residential care will appeal to both sets of readers. Despite the policy emphasis towards care in the community encoded in the NHS and Community Care Act 1990, residential care remains the bedrock service which is provided in practice for the frailest and most disabled older people in our society. As the book's authors say, residential care as both a concept and a practice has remained remarkably resistant to attempts fundamentally to change its purpose and form, or to abolish it. This despite some powerful academic critiques suggesting that its real function is to marginalize and segregate older people (see Townsend 1981), and the clear view of most older people that entering a residential home is very much a last resort, to be put off for as long as possible.

But if the residential home is still a major component in the practical care of older people – one which shows no signs of fading away – it nevertheless presents us in the late 1990s with certain paradoxes. These centre on questions about its true social function; whether it can be developed in new and more satisfying ways for older people; or whether it has become simply an outmoded form of care. Residential care is at a crossroads. Where does it go from here?

This book, which critically reviews the history of residential care and addresses such central questions, is therefore both timely and much needed. It is also one which its authors, Sheila Peace, Leonie Kellaher, and Dianne Willcocks, are eminently qualified to write, having been at the leading edge of the research of this topic throughout the 1980s and 1990s. Founding members of the Centre for Environmental and Social Studies in Ageing (CESSA), their research has focused on residential care and has been widely read and respected. As well as producing an impressive series of research publications and recommendations for policy and practice, they disseminated their findings through teaching, and pioneered practical initiatives such as *Inside Quality Assurance*, (CESSA 1992) which aimed to enhance the quality of residential provision.

Re-evaluating residential care is therefore firmly grounded in its authors' reflections on their own experience and knowledge, drawing on their 15 years of work in this subject area. It presents a comprehensive historical and contemporaneous survey of what is known about residential care and the people who live and work in residential homes. As gerontologists and social scientists, the authors follow this in Part Two of the book by addressing broad and fundamental questions about the future of residential care in our society, concluding with a discussion about how older people's sense of self and personal integrity may be preserved within the residential setting.

The book thus succeeds in achieving its authors' aims of providing a comprehensive re-evaluation of this important topic, one which is rooted in a detailed knowledge of the development of the residential home as both social policy and practice, and a critical assessment of its present and future role in age care.

Brian Gearing
School of Health and Social Welfare
The Open University

References

Centre for Environmental and Social Studies in Ageing (CESSA) (1992) *Inside Quality Assurance*. London: CESSA, University of North London.

Johnson, M.L. (1976) That was your life: a biographical approach to later life. In J.M.A. Munnichs and W.J.A. Van Den Heuval (eds), *Dependency or Interdependence in Old Age*. The Hague: Martinus Nijhoff.

Townsend, P. (1981) The structured dependency of the elderly: a creation of social policy in the twentieth century. *Ageing and Society*, 1: 5–28.

Walker, A. (1981) Towards a political economy of old age. *Ageing and Society*, 1: 73–94.

Preface

Residential care for older people is one of the most researched areas of social policy, and yet its role at the end of the twentieth century remains ambiguous. As researchers who have been at the forefront of such research throughout the 1980s and into the 1990s, we feel that it is time to stand back and take stock of what we know. It is common to hear the phrase 'old people want to stay in their own homes for as long as possible': why 'for as long as possible'? If we set this phrase aside we can ask why residential care persists, given that most older people want to remain in their own homes. We look for explanations for this paradox by examining the role of residential care and by asking the following questions.

- How far has the role of residential care been taken over by developments in nursing home care and sheltered housing? To what extent does residential care offer something unique in its own right?
- Does residential care continue to be a negative form of institutional care, one which in the main limits autonomy and personal choice, or is it a positive option for some older people?
- At the level of society, is residential care a symbol of the structured dependency of older people and a place where an ageist society can segregate those whose mental and physical decline offends? Or is residential care a symbol of society's concern for its frail members?
- Has residential care become an industry so tied up in the capital represented by bricks and mortar that it cannot be dismantled, or can it be complemented by domiciliary care?

These and other challenging questions form the basis of our re-evaluation of residential care. But they are first grounded in what we know about residential care through a detailed review of the facts and a critique of the research. Consequently, the book is in two distinct parts. Part I provides a comprehensive overview of the history of residential care, current provision and what is known about the everyday experience of older residents and those who work with them. Part II is devoted to three linked arguments which raise the questions outlined above.

Sheila Peace
Leonie Kellaher
Dianne Willcocks

Acknowledgements

Many people have been involved in the production of this book. We would like to thank Brian Gearing, Series Editor, and Jacinta Evans and Joan Malherbe at Open University Press for their continuing encouragement. A big thank you to Christian Schroeder at CESSA for producing the final script and remaining so good humoured. And to Tanya Hames at the School of Health and Social Welfare at the OU, for her presentation skills.

We are especially grateful to the following for their permission to reproduce text, diagrams and tables in this book: William Laing, Laing & Buisson; Maurice Heather, Phippen Randall and Parkes; Kent County Council Social Services Department; Counsel and Care; The Sainsbury Centre for Mental Health; Sage Publications; Tavistock Publications; Routledge, and the Department of Health.

Finally, to Tom, Amy and Steve who have lived with the box files for so long that they have come to regard them as part of the furniture – these things would not get done without you all.

PART I

Reviewing the knowledge

1

Past and present

A new book on old people's homes – what can we say that is genuinely 'new'? Social commentators on ageing are typically berated for describing the obvious in tedious detail; for developing modest incremental shifts within grandiose explanatory frameworks; and for failing to address fundamental aspects of change. These might be changes in ideology; changes in the social structure and demography of age; changes in professionalism; and cultural change around the status of older people in contemporary society. This book, a re-evaluation of residential care, aims to locate institutional living within these changing events. Some exploration of familiar territory will be necessary, against a shifting back cloth of evidence and experience. Beyond this, the authors will challenge those myths and misperceptions around residential care that have blocked previous attempts to unsettle an unsatisfactory status quo.

In an earlier text (Willcocks *et al.* 1987) we refer to a catalogue of 'unfinished business' surrounding the conceptualization and development of accommodation and care, and we focus attention on a series of practical impediments to change. These turn around the arbitrary boundaries and the uncomfortable relationships between life in the community and life in a home. Particularly, we considered the kind of physical form that would promote a domain akin to home; and the kind of resident-centred regime that would foster a sense of homeness, alongside a programme of development and incentives to inculcate appropriate skills, attitudes and competencies among care staff. Over and above these issues, *Private Lives in Public Places* made concrete suggestions as to the kind of arrangements that would give primacy to public accountability and community involvement within this increasingly differentiated world of residential care homes which spans public, private and voluntary sectors.

In the present book we hope to advance our somewhat gloomy prognostication, written in 1987, which reads:

In the absence of . . . a critical review and re-evaluation of the role and structure of residential care, our best endeavours to deal with haunting memories of the past are doomed to failure. Minor adjustments will not suffice to shift the balance of institutional control. If residential homes continue to serve as a substantial part of the care spectrum, then an improved residential response must be constructed; one that will acknowledge and compensate for the powerlessness of older people who are presently obliged to submit without question to society's caring solutions.

(Willcocks et al. 1987: 170–1)

Defining residential care

We might begin by asking what residential care is? A rational account would perhaps offer the following: a social or collective response to different individual, family or group requirements for accommodation that provides care, continuity and opportunities for living in ways that are socially, culturally and spatially acceptable and affordable.

In other words, residential care is acknowledged to be a complex phenomenon which defies simple explanation – and, as is often the case where complexity exists, there is a tendency for simple truths to be promulgated which mask uncomfortable realities. In this instance, it is the everyday accounts of those who live and work in residential settings which remain unspoken. It is perhaps not surprising that many critiques of residential living which have promoted discussion and debate around care arrangements in later life have failed to address simple definitional questions or progressed towards an analysis of residential living which would make sense in terms of the day-to-day world of residents and their carers. We will argue that, for many, there is a gross mismatch between expressed intent and outcome. This argument forms a major theme for this text.

Reflection reminds us that we 'know' certain things about residential care. We 'know' that it is typically regarded as the contemporary expression of institutional living whose roots can be traced, in a relatively linear fashion, back to the nineteenth-century Poor Law and the associated workhouses, regarded by latter-day social commentators with a mixture of fear and loathing (Webb and Webb 1910; 1927; Townsend 1962). What we also 'know' from political, professional and intellectual outsiders is that the major interventions in the social, physical and ideological fabric of institutional living have tended to be made manifest through changes in form rather than function, for example, the development of 'small-group living', or the development of the multi-purpose residential unit (Peace 1986). What we also 'know', but, it may be argued, generally choose not to know, is that a silence persists about the essence of residential living – a silence on the part of those older people who may never enter residential care, but for whom the institutional option casts a shadow of deep anxiety and uncertainty in later life, as they fear its imminence; and a silence on the part of those who do actually cross the threshold into care.

Contrasted with the silence of the older person is the noisy intervention of the media observers who play out an occasional scenario of neglect and abuse that contributes to the external view of the residential home but fails to give a meaningful voice to those who live out their lives in care settings, for example see 'Ending Up' (*The Guardian.* Bennett, October 1994). So perhaps our earlier definition of residential care should be subject to challenge. It must be informed by the ideas and experiences of those for whom life in residential care becomes significant: present and potential residents and their carers.

Perspectives on residential care

Beyond the user perspective, there are other frameworks which we must take into account. If we accept the criticism (Baldwin *et al.* 1993) that empirical research on residential care in the 1980s neglected wider structural factors in its analysis, we need to reconsider the notion articulated by Townsend (1981) of society devising for its elders, either deliberately or unknowingly, a form of structured dependency and question whether we have moved beyond even this analysis. Baldwin *et al.* suggest that too much emphasis was placed upon the internal workings of the residential setting and the strictly delimited range of actions and roles available to people once they had entered residential care, and that the influence of Goffman's concept of 'total institutions' was pervasive. They state that we (the authors), along with others, ignored the context that permits or requires homes to function at all. Their 'defence' of residential homes follows a line of argument that older people have an induced dependency, whether or not they enter residential care, because of economic and social structures in the wider society which foster dependency for older people. They argue persuasively that the residential setting is not to blame. This debate, involving the juxtaposition of different schools of thought, will form a major theme of Part Two of this book.

Putting aside notions of 'blame' we are, nevertheless, faced with the task of unravelling and understanding a mass of evidence, not least from our own earlier and more recent research. What does this tell us about residential care in the aftermath of the community care legislation of the early 1990s – the most fundamental rethink and reorganization of care service infrastructure for older people since the post-war optimism deriving from Beveridge? In the past decade, there have been many changes, not least in terms of the changing profile for providers of residential care. This has influenced the characteristics of those who live and work in homes; those who own and/or manage homes and those who make judgements about standards and 'quality'. Moreover, there are changes to the notion of contract between the care provider and the customer – whether that customer is an older person or an informal carer. Equally, there have been developments in understandings about the diversity of older people as receivers of care and their relationships with both informal and formal care givers across a range of settings. All of these topics will be addressed critically through a detailed profile of residential care at the end of the millennium. Here we would wish to make the point that, notwithstanding certain key shifts over time, there are also remarkable consistencies. A charting of this historical development forms the major task of this first chapter.

A legacy of care: Victorian values

Embedded in popular consciousness is a set of images around the 'workhouse' – accepted unquestioningly as the legitimate Victorian antecedent of today's residential home. Just what does this mean? Students of social history are familiar with a scenario whereby, under the 1834 Poor Law arrangements, those without employment, money or shelter, and those who were sick and without family support, were obliged to seek 'relief'. This was offered as 'outdoor relief' by means of a minimal payment, sufficiently modest to ensure that the fate of a person receiving it should be worse than that of the lowest grade of self-supporting labourer. Alternatively, it might be offered as 'indoor relief' within the workhouse, where people of widely varying origin and capability were required to labour for their keep. Accounts from the workhouse testify graphically to the crudeness of these arrangements. According to Thompson:

> Middle-class visitors entering a workhouse for the first time could be deeply shaken by the harsh indignity of the prison-like routine, the grotesque, despairing and toothless faces, 'the forlorn, half-dazed aspect of these battered human hulks who were once young'. There was no need to write up the words 'abandon hope all ye who enter here'. George Lansbury [(1928: 135–6)] wrote of the Poplar workhouse, 'The place was clean: brass knobs and floors were polished, but of goodwill, kindliness there was none'.
>
> (Thompson *et al.* 1990: 37)

The poor relief response was designed around the principle of 'lesser eligibility' and founded on a notion of causality that carefully balanced economic and moral factors; here, the language of fecklessness and idleness vied for supremacy with evidence that prevailing economic structures and capacity simply could not sustain the whole population in productive and self-help activity. In a situation at the turn of the century where increasing numbers of the population were found to be 'pauperized', the tendency to blame the poor – a tendency which may be familiar to those who have experienced the recent renewal of Victorian values – sustained a set of arguments that it was simply not possible for the nation to feed and clothe those who could not or would not provide for themselves.

With a falling mortality rate and an increase in absolute numbers of old people in the latter decades of the nineteenth century – coupled with an increasing propensity on the part of employers to link ageing with reduced efficiency and to lay off workers in their sixties – it soon became apparent that there were increasing numbers of respectable and meritorious indigents for whom separate provision was required. Such provision was away from the residuum at the bottom of society for whom punitive measures were constructed in order to engender socially acceptable behaviours. For older people, separate provision offered privileges and 'comforts', typically in separate wings of the old workhouses. Comfort meant the wearing of one's own clothes; being able to go on visits; or sharing a room with your spouse – an important set of ameliorations to a miserable existence.

The early twentieth century

Ideologically, the emergence of a labour movement and the development of liberal and socialist philosophy form a crucial underpinning to developing ideas around social and political intervention. However, the impact of these new movements on the daily lives of older people in the workhouse was slow in coming. A major focus for reformists was family life and the need to support the unemployed, the sick and children. Unspoken assumptions about the family prevailed, with an expectation that older family members would benefit from general improvements in family life.

When the Royal Commission on the Poor Laws (1909) reported, some 140,000 older people were resident in Poor Law institutions, representing almost half the institutional population. The report coincided with a growing awareness of the incidence of poverty, as noted in the seminal works of Booth (1899) and Rowntree (1910), and an understanding that vulnerable groups, such as older people, could not manage without additional support – hence the 1908 Old Age Pensions Act. Imperceptibly, the social construction of retirement was beginning.

Writing in 1962, Townsend observes that during the period between 1910 and 1946, the public accepted the drawing of a veil over institutional arrangements for their elders. There was a conspicuous absence of official inquiries and reports, and he comments that the 'few fleeting references to their circumstances and their needs amounted to a conspiracy of silence on the subject' (Townsend 1962: 27). The significant, if understated, change during this period was the reclassification of the various institutions and a transfer of governing powers in 1929 from the Poor Law Board of Governors to county and borough councils. The outcome was the Public Assistance Institution – soon to come under scrutiny by the wartime Nuffield Survey (Means and Smith 1985).

The burgeoning welfare state

Popular wisdom tells us that the experiences of struggling together against a common enemy in war-torn Britain encouraged communities to rethink the values of traditional social hierarchies and to support the challenge for a more just and caring society that was implicit in the electoral campaign of the Labour Party in 1945. It is evident that the war years were characterized by a number of substantial social and political interventions which were to culminate in the adoption of the term 'welfare state' to encapsulate developments in education policy, in housing, in social and health policies and in social security. The essential background to these changes was expressed powerfully by Beveridge, who interpreted a simple brief to tidy up pensions as a mandate for developing a vision of society that was more socially just, more materially equal and more truly democratic. This he achieved in his 1942 report which was to inform a consensus on the social contract between government and people for the next four decades (Beveridge 1942).

Older people were to be found at the heart of these changes – in particular, with respect to aspirations for improved access to health care, pensions and appropriate housing. So when the Nuffield Survey on Public Assistance Institutions reported in 1947, the Labour government felt able to make a forthright statement highlighting the poor and harsh conditions in which old people were then living and to propose major changes to future residential provision (Nuffield Foundation 1947). The reporting committee identified major concerns about the scale of individual institutions. There was an implicit assumption that an inappropriate regime was a function of inappropriate (and over-large) size of the residential establishment. The report argued that 'all normal old people who are no longer able to lead an independent life should be accommodated in small Homes rather than in large institutions' (quoted in Townsend 1962: 31).

This could not be achieved at once, but 'several thousand' homes were said to be required over a period of 15–20 years. These sentiments were echoed by the Minister of Health, Aneurin Bevan, when he introduced the National Assistance Bill in 1947:

> We have decided to make a great departure in the treatment of old people. The workhouse is to go. Although many people have tried to humanise it, it was in many respects a very evil institution. We have determined that the right way to approach this problem is to give the Welfare Authorities, as we shall now describe them, the power to establish separate homes ... If we have an institution too large, we might have a reproduction of the workhouse atmosphere ... and all the regimentation and the rules that have to be obeyed, and therefore it seems to us that the optimum limit for these homes must be 25 or 30 persons.
>
> (quoted in Townsend 1962: 32)

The annual report of the Ministry of Health (MoH) in 1948–9 included the following words 'The old master and inmate relationship is being replaced by one nearly approaching that of hotel manager and his guests' (MoH 1950: 311). Furthermore, Section 21 of the National Assistance Act 1948 placed a duty on local authorities to provide 'residential accommodation for persons who, by reason of age, infirmity or any other circumstances are in need of care and attention not otherwise available to them'. This represents a formal commitment to the social contract whereby the state would provide for people at times of need, and it signalled an important move forward in terms of the 'welfare consensus'.

Sadly, aligning rhetoric with reality was not a straightforward matter. In the 1950s building materials were in short supply and, typically, old people's homes were created from upgraded workhouses and old, converted buildings (Means and Smith 1985). A particular challenge was to reclassify provision between hospital and residential services, especially in relation to older people who were also chronically sick. In 1948 there were 400 public assistance institutions (PAIs) which accommodated some 130,000 people. During that year a gradual splitting of provision took place, and 100 PAIs were transferred to the MoH for use as hospitals; a further 100 went to local authorities for use as residential homes; and the remaining 200 were for 'joint user establishments' (MoH 1949).

So the 'hotel model' remained a distant vision. Not for the first time – or indeed the last – concerns about the 'ageing of the population' raised fears about costs and the need for economies of scale. This led to the suggestion in 1954 that homes would have to accommodate 60 residents (MoH 1955), reversing earlier arguments; accordingly, debates over the distinction between hospital and residential care and the scale of provision rumbled on (see Peace 1986). And while the 1948 National Assistance Act gave local authorities the powers to offer support to residents within private and voluntary homes, and to register such homes, their numbers remained small compared with the growing public sector provision .

What we have little sense of during this time is what older residents thought of these developments and how the public responded. Looking back half a century at the way in which a confident Labour administration set out its grand design for a comprehensive care infrastructure – 'from the cradle to the grave' – a range of social commentators are now asking the simple question: what went wrong? Vulnerable groups in society, including older people, have failed to benefit from state welfare in the way that was intended, and evidence of stress and distress in our social system persists. Where does the form of social response we call residential care fit into this picture?

Radicals and reformists

Not until the late 1940s and early 1950s did the unacceptable face of institutional care become a suitable subject for political and intellectual debate, to be addressed by social commentators of substance. The conspiracy of silence from governmental bodies referred to by Townsend with respect to the first part of the twentieth century was replicated among scholars for the first fifteen years of the post-war consensus. The complacency which generated the slogan 'You've never had it so good' was punctured by the 'rediscovery of poverty' in the early 1960s with the writings of those such as Townsend (1957) and Coates and Silburn (1970). Then came a groundswell of debate and writing about the societal role of institutions, particularly in relation to mental hospitals and prisons. Radical theory emerged in the literature from Europe and the USA, from such eminent researchers, philosophers and practitioners as Barton (1959), Goffman (1961), Foucault (1967) and Szasz (1961). They set out to undermine the idea of the institution as a place of reform. While Foucault and Szasz conceptualized mental hospitals as places of repression and social control, Barton and Goffman focused on people and the experience of incarceration – exploring, vividly, those processes of depersonalization which can take place within institutions.

In the field of mental health this was a time of mass deinstitutionalization in the USA and the first hesitant soundings around the development of community care policies in Britain. An increase in the use of behaviour modification and drug therapy sat uncomfortably alongside a greater focus on the rights of patients (see Jones and Fowles 1984). These changes and debates were to have a profound influence on institutional provision for all sectors of society. They were not, however, the central concerns for Townsend. The most influential empirical study of residential care for older people in a century of debate and deliberation, *The Last Refuge*, remains unchallenged to this day in terms of its power to chart the unacceptable face of society's response to older people. Townsend's work is rooted in the social reformist and empirical tradition within British social policy, and it set out to discover whether the system of residential care for older people which had replaced the Poor Law was the right one. The answer was, in the event, a resounding 'no!'.

> The blunt fact is that the government has tried to abandon the policies of the Poor Law without sufficiently considering the alternative policies that should take their place. It is no less than astonishing that in the middle of the twentieth century new policies can be introduced and after a decent interval modified, without detailed inquiry into both the best use of existing buildings and the needs and wishes of persons living there. At no time has there been any official attempt to instigate such an enquiry and to review post-war developments.
>
> (Townsend 1962: 39)

Townsend wanted to know how, and which, older people entered institutions; and what alternatives should exist. He was less concerned with care practices in residential homes and how these might be improved. Analysis was centred around the importance of family life and of patterns of reciprocity among family members. Townsend saw the questions raised by the idea of a residential home as part of much wider policy changes which would be needed as a proper structure for the support of older people.

The principles of care he espoused were expressed as: self-determination, respect for the individual; maintenance of health; preservation of residential independence; right to an occupation; social security; social opportunity; security of income; and social equality. Within this positive framework Townsend explored the purpose of the residential home with a degree of ambivalence:

> The role of the residential institution or Home in a general policy designed to give effect to these principles is uncertain. Is it to be a permanent refuge for infirm persons who cannot care for themselves in a home of their own, who cannot be supported in their homes by any practicable system of domiciliary services, and who yet are not in need of continuous nursing care and medical treatment in hospital? Is it to be a temporary refuge for frail persons recovering from illness or malnutrition or seeking to give relatives or workers in the domiciliary services a hard earned rest or perhaps a chance of improving the facilities available at home? Or is it to simply be a rescue device for the present generation of old people whose differing needs cannot be met because good housing, adequate pensions, and comprehensive local domiciliary services are not yet provided? Many of the inherent contradictions in present policy spring from a failure to explore or attempt to answer these questions.
>
> (Townsend 1962: 388)

Specific recommendations followed which eliminated the need for communal homes. These included the development of sheltered and specially designed housing; the creation of a strong domiciliary care service to support people and their families within their own homes; better medical services for older people; the reduction of communal homes; the transference to the National Health Service of responsibilty for establishments catering for incapacitated and chronically sick old persons who, for the time being, cannot be given adequate medical and nursing care in their own homes; short-stay accommodation; and the regulation of private and voluntary homes – all this was an urgent agenda for action, in 1962 (Townsend 1962: 386–429). The negative views expressed by Townsend regarding future possibilities for residential care came directly from his research, in which he encountered residents who had experienced:

> Loss of occupation; isolation from family, friends and community; the tenuousness of new relationships with other residents and staff; the loneliness; loss of privacy and identity; and the collapse of powers of self-determination.
>
> (Townsend 1962: 338)

The 1960s and 1970s

The two decades following this major work saw only tentative and piecemeal developments along the lines prescribed by Townsend. There was no coherent overarching policy framework for older people which made the connections between pensions, housing, social welfare and health. But initially, the social contract remained firmly in place (if lacking in public scrutiny). During the 1960s, the major emphasis in policy statements from the Ministry of Health was on the development of community care through extended and improved domiciliary care, health and other welfare services. The 1962 Building Note reinforced the analogy of the 'domestic home' as a model for institutional care (MoH 1962). There was an increasing emphasis on providing residential care for a group labelled the 'frail elderly'; and the debate continued over who should be providing continuing nursing care for older people (Means and Smith 1985). Regulations were introduced concerning the conduct of homes in the private and voluntary sectors (Statutory Instruments 1962 No 2000), and the 1968 Health Services and Public Health Act enabled local authorities to arrange for provision of accommodation in private homes.

A significant policy development came in the late 1960s with the publication of guidance by Ministry of Housing and Local Government (1969) on the further development of housing for older people and codified the beginnings of sheltered housing initiatives within the public sector. The familiar distinctions were made:

> Category One consisted of purpose-built flats or bungalows with a warden, but often with no common room or other facilities for shared use; Category Two was usually identified as a scheme with individual bungalows or flats linked by heated internal corridors. A common room, laundry and guest room and other facilities for shared use are normally included.
>
> (Mackintosh *et al.* 1990: 87)

However, policy related to sheltered housing was developed (at the Ministry of Housing and Local Government, later the Department of the Environment) quite independently from that of residential provision (which remained in a different government department, at the Ministry of Health, which became the Department of Health and Social Security). Indeed sheltered housing was conceived, in the first instance, as a response to the needs of council house dwellers and their concerned local authority landlords – where they were no longer seen to need (or justify) the space of the family home; and where, in their later years, they might require the assistance of a warden who would take on the role of a good neighbour (Mackintosh *et al.* 1990; Means 1991).

Meanwhile, the scale of residential living was increasing. By 1970 there were some 128,209 persons over the age of 65 years living in residential homes in England: 86,857 (68 per cent) in local authority homes; 23,262 (18 per cent) in homes run by the voluntary sector; and 18,090 (14 per cent) in private sector homes (Department of Health and Social Security (DHSS) 1971). This represented approximately 2 per cent of the population aged over 65, shown at the 1971 census to be 7.2 million persons. Local authorities built some 100 new homes that year, accommodating 4,544 residents; and 14 former PAIs were able to close (DHSS 1971). But policy started to favour the development of domiciliary care; there was an early optimism that this would enable older people, with the help of their families, to remain within their own homes as long as possible. In April 1971, the 1968 Health Services and Public Health Act was brought into force and Circular 19/71 explained the new powers that would promote the welfare of old people – albeit within the bounds of what was deemed to be affordable – that is, the cost of sustaining older people moved back centre stage (DHSS 1972a).

The Circular recognized that shortage of resources would limit authorities to:

> gradual development, but it gave general authorisation to inform elderly people of the range of services available and to identify those in need; to provide social work support, advisory, visiting, meals and recreational services and facilities (and transport to use them); to arrange for schemes of supervised lodgings and to support warden service schemes in the public and private sectors. Further extension would later be possible.
>
> (DHSS 1972a: 32)

So community services expanded at a measured pace, with 473,900 households receiving home help in 1972 – of whom 85 per cent were older people (DHSS 1973: 32). Local authority social services and housing budgets were still generally growing until around 1973–4 and national targets were developed for numbers of home helps per 1,000 population. At the same time, attention turned to the targeting of residential accommodation for the most dependent old people. Older people with dementia were identified as a potentially large group within psychiatric hospitals. Accordingly, any reduction in long-stay mental health institutions would imply new accommodation for older people emerging from such establishments at the rate of 2.5–3 beds per 1,000 population aged 65 or over (DHSS 1972a; 1973). Moreover, adequate day facilities would also be needed. While a small number of purpose-built residential homes for older people with mental health problems had already been constructed, the question of volume had not been fully addressed. Meanwhile, the influence of new research such as *Taken for a Ride* (Meacher 1972) and, subsequently, *The Rising Tide* (Health Advisory Service 1982) placed the needs of older people with mental health problems firmly within the residential debate. Predictions about the demography of an ageing population and the incidence of dementing illnesses in extreme old age began to command serious attention among key policy-makers. These trends were reflected in issues of design. The 1973 revision of the DHSS Building Note took on board the growing complexities of residential living; the needs of different groups of long-stay residents; the move to a multi-purpose home with the introduction of day care, short stay and meals services; the importance of community interactions; the breaking down of large spaces into groups or family units; and the needs of residents for both greater privacy and self determination (DHSS and Welsh Office 1973).

The issue of care practices began to move to the fore and it is here that the influence of academic work on the effects of institutionalization is seen to have filtered through to social planners (see, for example, Hanson 1972). In 1973, the Personal Social Services Council (PSSC) was established to replace various advisory bodies in the field of social care. Its remit was to advise ministers on policy issues and to provide an information and advice service based on projects sponsored by the Council (DHSS 1975). The debate about residential care practice began to accelerate. In 1974 the PSSC set up a working party to examine standards and, simultaneously, the DHSS Social Work Development Group set up a project to examine the philosophy of residential care – with particular questions about the use of new, purpose-built residential homes that had also been planned to provide day care (DHSS 1975). Bodies such as these produced a series of influential documents on practice issues throughout the late 1970s, including *Residential Care Reviewed* (PSSC 1977). However, residential practice and residential policy remained isolated from the wider development of community-based services for older people and their families. While residential care might be spoken of as part of the hypothetical continuum of care, it still remained distinct and was viewed in a different light. And yet the lives of substantial numbers of older people were subject to the authority of residential arrangements: in 1976, for the population of those aged 65 or more, 99,000 were in public sector homes; 33,000 in voluntary homes (of which 14,000 were supported); and 27,000 in private homes (of which 2,000 were supported) (DHSS 1977). This represents an investment from public funds, channelled through local authorities, with respect to 115,000 elderly people.

Inevitably and blatantly, the issue of 'affordability' came to assume dominance as the decade progressed. Costly programmes of public intervention came under close scrutiny. And a victory for the populist campaign of Margaret Thatcher in 1979 was not unconnected with her restatement of individual responsibility; the continuing role of the family; and the reclamation of Victorian values of probity, endeavour and thrift.

Opening up the market

The late 1970s and the election of the Thatcher government in 1979 were to herald an era of change in the fortunes of older people. Those who had prudently made appropriate and private provision for their later years were to be praised and rewarded with choice and opportunity. Those who had been seduced, by a lifetime's contribution to National Insurance, into thinking that the reciprocal obligations between society and its members might now be realized, were to suffer a rude awakening. Society, we were told in the 1980s, no longer existed. The experience of radical change for older people merits sober reflection.

In 1978 the Labour government had introduced as a discussion document, *A Happier Old Age*, proposing a framework which protected the status quo and indicating that the legitimate needs of an ageing population would mean a growth in services – including residential services – during a period of generalized financial constraint (DHSS and Welsh Office 1978). Regrettably, this positive message did not survive, and the Conservative victory in 1979 triggered the break-up of what is generally accepted as a tacit post-war consensus between the political parties concerning welfare provision. The philosophical vacuum was soon to be filled through the introduction of New Right thinking based on free market principles which took us beyond consensus to a new-style conflict between parties with vested interests. Service provision was to become increasingly open to a mixed economy of providers, responding to the assumed needs of 'consumers', and privatization was to be the buffer that would protect the economically active from unreasonable demands on the public purse.

The White Paper *Growing Older* (DHSS 1981) gave an indication of many of the central planks of the Conservative programme. It returned unashamedly to the emphasis of the positive aspects of family life, and the support which should be given by families for their older members. At the same time, it introduced the concept of a service user as a 'consumer' of services who had 'rights' to certain types of control over services.

Behind the rhetoric of politicians, there was developing an increasing knowledge and understanding of the prevailing culture and capability of the residential care sector that was to underpin significant changes in patterns of provision. In the early 1980s a number of strands converged. First, there was the growing body of research-based data concerning life in residential homes. In the early 1980s the DHSS and other bodies commissioned a number of substantial pieces of research on local authority residential homes – see Judge and Sinclair (1986) for an overview, plus Davies and Knapp (1981) and Booth (1985). It is important to record that at the turn of the decade most residential beds were in the public sector. In the main, the research was aimed at improving residential care practice; it sought to understand how the design of homes could be improved and how residents could inform the design process (Willcocks *et al.* 1982; 1987); it looked at how the needs of mentally ill older people could best be served (Wilkin and Jolley 1979; Evans *et al.* 1981); it considered changes in the mental and physical health of residents over time and whether or not regimes in homes could be different (Booth 1985); it looked at the costs of residential care (Knapp 1981); it sought to understand how residents arrived in homes and the process of admission (Lawrence *et al.* 1987; Neill *et al.* 1988); and it explored the overlap between different forms of provision in caring for frail older people (Godlove *et al.* 1982; Wade *et al.* 1983).

What this body of research did not challenge was the role of residential care as an instrument of social policy. Rather, its outcome was concerned with working to develop residential care and improve upon it. This period of research activity is characterized by an innovative and developmental approach to research methodology. The work of Goffman on 'institutionaliz-ation' and other earlier writers was influential – but so, too, were develop-ments in systems theory, production of welfare models, 'quality of life' indicators, and more qualitative methods which sought to understand the interactions between individuals and the processes which linked them and the environments in which they lived and worked (Peace 1993a). For the first time, the complexities of the residential world were examined using multi-method approaches and the possibilities of 'triangulation' were explored (Kellaher and Peace 1990).

But even as this work was beginning to filter into practice (for example, through staff training and the design of new homes), the nature of residential care was undergoing radical change. At a superficial level, this change is cap-tured by a dramatic set of statistics. In 1976, figures for England show that there was only one person accommodated in a private residential home for every five in public sector homes (21,320 compared with 99,027); by 1982 this ratio had changed dramatically to one in three (35,839 compared with 103,720); by 1988 the ratio was almost exactly one to one, and from 1989 onwards the balance tipped the other way, with the private sector dominat-ing residential provision (Laing 1995). Figures for 1992 show that for every resident in a local authority home there were now two in private care. What this demonstrates is that alongside the deregulation of public transport, the sell-off of public utilities and the 'downsizing' of traditional industries in Britain, the care industry would also develop (and be 'encouraged') in accord-ance with market principles.

Undoubtedly, there has been an increase in the number and proportion of older people between 75 and 85 years; and this, typically, is the age group which dominates the residential population. Yet between 1981 and 1991 the residential population grew at a much faster rate than the older population. This suggests that an explanation for the increase in numbers of homes is likely to lie somewhere between political ideology and demographics.

Reviewing residential care

It was during this period of intense sectoral change that the (then) Secretary of State for Health and Social Services, Norman Fowler, commissioned an Independent Review of Residential Care in order that the sector might 'respond effectively to changing social needs' (National Institute for Social Work 1988a: 1). Set up at a time 'when there was a wide agreement that resi-dential services, particularly in the statutory sector, were in a demoralised state, too often used as a service of last resort and seen to be of low status'

(NISW 1988a: 1), the Wagner report, as it became known, made some 45 recommendations covering a wide range of policy and practice issues – for example, making an informed choice about accommodation and services; the rights of residents; complaints procedures, regulatory frameworks, staff training and recognition; and the needs of people from minority ethnic groups (NISW 1988a). While some of these recommendations were brought within the legislative framework of the NHS and Community Care Act 1990, other aspects of practice were the subject of demonstration projects carried out under the Caring in Homes Initiative which ran from 1989 to 1992 (Youll and McCourt-Perring 1993).

Community care legislation and its consequences

The fragility of financial arrangements supporting residential care – for the provider, for the customer and for the public purse – was self-evident. The late 1980s saw a period of immense debate about the 'perverse incentives' towards residential care, especially for older people, and weighty statements were made regarding the need to control public finance in this area (Audit Commission 1986; DHSS 1987; Griffiths 1988; DoH 1989a; and the NHS and Community Care Act 1990). As a result, from April 1993, local authorities took over the role of handling the funding which can be made available to persons without adequate means who are assessed as being in need of residential and nursing home care.

The logic of this shift of responsibility was to link care needs with a cash response. It was intended that the decision to go into residential care should be made as part of a process of assessment which considers the wishes of service users (and their carers) and the range of alternative community care services which may be available. In principle, a place may be found within a home in any sector. In practice, the availability of resources to support appropriate outcomes has often been found to be lacking (Wistow 1995). In essence, the community care reforms of the 1980s and 1990s have encouraged local authorities to create an 'internal market' for service purchasing and providing, and this had led many authorities to contract with private and voluntary home owners for their services. In addition, many former local authority homes have now been contracted out to the independent sector.

Changes in the family and the visibility of carers

Alongside evidence of the restructuring of formal care arrangements as a result of state intervention is the visible transformation of what is termed the informal care sector – that is to say, the family or, more simply, women and their changing role and circumstances. The increase in the numbers of older people living in residential care homes coincides with changes in the nature of women's employment and in women's expectations in other areas. This in turn is linked to an increase in the divorce rate and the reformulation of living arrangements. All of these affect the nature of family life. While the government has placed emphasis on the care of older people within the family, such trends must be acknowledged and accommodated if care in the family is to be a reliable and viable contributor to the range of care alternatives. Indeed, care within families has been provided for decades. It is now more visible than ever. Throughout the 1980s writers, many of them feminist writers, focused attention on the experience of carers and the imperative to recognize their needs (Finch and Groves 1983; Lewis and Meredith 1988; Qureshi and Walker 1989). While initial work in this area concentrated on women as carers, ongoing research has defined the diversity of carers, especially the role of spouses caring for older partners and the growing number of male carers in this category (Arber and Ginn 1990; 1991; Twigg *et al.* 1990).

In the context of enhancing service provision for frail older people, such research has highlighted the need for partnership between older people, informal and formal carers. In addition, it calls for a recognition of the complex dynamics that exist between different sets of wishes (Allen *et al.* 1992). The renewed emphasis and shifting interpretation of community care services throughout the late 1980s and into the 1990s has thrown these dynamics into sharp relief. As the profile of local services is developed within the framework of the NHS and the Community Care Act 1990, many families are finding that community care services remain piecemeal, inflexible and an increasingly expensive alternative to family care. In these circumstances, residential care is construed as a necessary option from the carer's perspective, and it also seems inevitable for the older person by virtue of the constrained choices which characterize the formal response to need.

Another compelling set of contributory factors relates to the manner in which older people and their families pay for long-term care. Poverty has long been a reason for some older people finding themselves subject to the institutional 'solution'; hence they become resident in residential care. Authors such as Walker (1993) have drawn our attention to the fact that, while some older people are much better off, many old people today continue to live on very low incomes, and this is particularly true of older women and working-class families. In recent years, older women have represented the main clientele for all forms of residential care.

> Like all good myths, the myth of affluence in old age has some basis in reality. While there has only been a slight relative improvement in the incomes of the majority of pensioners, for some the increase has been substantial – giving rise to the so-called WOOPIE, or well-off older person. The 'two-nations' in old age, forewarned by Titmuss (1963) thirty years ago are now firmly entrenched at the extremes of the income distribution, with a third group making up the bulk of low-income pensioners. Differences based on class, age, gender, race and marital status are reflected in income inequalities and, at the extremes are younger (60–74) middle-class males and married couples, and older (75+) women and working-class families.
>
> (Walker 1993: 287)

Differential housing tenure is another factor in the equation of cost and care. As a result of a dramatic transformation of tenure patterns in Britain since the 1960s, there is a much greater probability that, at the point of retirement, an individual will be an owner occupier (Thorns 1994; Hamnett 1995). In

1945 there were 3 million homeowners in Britain, 25 per cent of all British households. By 1970 this had increased to 50 per cent, and by 1994–5 to 66 per cent (Office of Population Censuses and Surveys (OPCS) 1996).

However, while the British may have become a nation of homeowners, the equity held in housing stock and the quality of that stock vary dramatically across the country, and are related to the vagaries of the housing market (Hamnett *et al.* 1991; Forrest *et al.* 1990). The case has been made that, rather than owner-occupation leading to a redistribution of wealth (Saunders 1990), it has led to the maintenance of the status quo (Hamnett 1995). Nevertheless, in relation to funding long-term care for older people, it does mean that more and more people are funding their own care through the sale of their housing. In recent times the effects which paying for care may have on opportunities for inheritance between family members has been set alongside proposals for the future funding of long-term care through pensions systems. However, as we have noted for many older women and members of minority ethnic groups, a lack of pension cover and poverty in old age remain crucial in the choice of care setting in advanced old age.

Changes in long-term care

Alongside the shifts in social housing and the impact on older people's stake in the property market is a shift in the reconceptualization of long-term care around the need for clinical support – and thereby, a challenge to the stake of older people in hospital provision (Hunter 1992). A demand for alternative forms of long-term care is associated with increasing pressure on hospitals from those older people who do not require specialist services but do require intensive caring. In 1987, the Firth report showed that since 1979 there had been little change in the occupancy rates for geriatric beds, and its authors expressed concern that, given the increase in numbers of the population aged 75 years and over, the balance of long-term care had shifted elsewhere (DHSS 1987: 86). Since that time the picture has changed, with the increasing decline in geriatric beds. According to a survey among community health councils by the Association of Community Health Councils for England and Wales (1990), 77 per cent reported a reduction in the provision of continuing care beds between 1987 and 1990. In addition, district health authorities were not replacing their facilities by contracting beds in private nursing homes; rather, older people were supported within the independent sector either through social security payments or through self-financing.

Since April 1993, the situation has become more complex as local authorities have taken over the main responsibility for the assessment and financing of older people in both residential and nursing homes. Meanwhile, health authorities continue to have responsibility for providing a long-term care service and may still contract places in nursing homes, and joint eligibility criteria for the assessment of continuing health care needs are presently being put into place (DoH 1995a). Finally, the actual and proposed closure of a number of large-scale psychiatric hospitals means that a diverse group of older people with behavioural and/or mental health problems must be offered alternative forms of accommodation along with varying levels of support.

A question of quality

While the providers of residential care changed dramatically during the course of the 1980s, concern over standards of care and the quality of care persisted. Elsewhere we have traced the development of the formal regulatory framework which has evolved for residential and nursing home care since the early part of this century (Kellaher *et al.* 1988; DoH and Welsh Office 1990). An early critique and contribution to the quality debate is seen in work of the Personal Social Services Council, where a Residential Care Working Party identified a need to consolidate legislation covering the registration of private and voluntary homes. In the wake of the Townsend statements on care there was an acknowledgement that accountabilities were piecemeal and not comprehensive, that there was a failure to specify care standards, and that the need for a system of registration and approval (or inspection) was in no way diminished (PSSC 1977: 22–30).

The sense of urgency became marked with the rapid 1980s expansion of the independent sector. Hence, following consolidating legislation and discussion of the guidance document, *A Good Home* (DHSS and Welsh Office, 1982), the present system of registration and inspection was codified in the Registered Homes Act 1984 and in its accompanying regulations (see Kellaher *et al.* 1988: 19). The recent history of the development of regulatory practice is continued in Chapter 2.

In summary, then, we have charted a century of piecemeal change throughout which residential care remains a central plank of the care provision available to older people at the end of their lives. Yet its meaning remains ambiguous – viewed with a mix of loathing, resignation, guilt, acceptance, anticipation and pragmatism on the part of older people and their families, the general public and politicians. Whether it remains the ultimate symbol of the way our society devalues older people or has yet to develop its potential as a form of humane care outside the family home for those who choose it, is central to the debate in Part Two of this book. In the rest of Part One we continue to look at facts and findings about the people and places which make up residential care and current developments in residential practice.

2

People and places

The recent past has witnessed a dramatic expansion of care provision, and the realignment of procedures consequent upon the NHS and Community Care Act. This has been accompanied by a growing body of data providing analysis of the trends in long-term care for older people (Laing 1995). The body of factual knowledge arising from such a history adds to our understanding of the practical parameters of residential care since the 1988 publication of the Wagner report, *A Positive Choice* (NISW 1988a). In this chapter, we review this information about changing residential trends and populations in order to discuss the people involved in residential care and the homes in which they live and work. In answering the questions 'why these people?', 'why in these places?', we aim to shed further light on the ways in which, for certain older people, residential care becomes the most practical option. In other words, the match between profiles of residents and their present living arrangements, and the profile of staff and their present employment, can be explained as more than mere contingency. We start by reviewing the changes which have taken place in and around residential care homes over the 15 years since we wrote our account of 100 local authority residential homes for older people (Willcocks *et al.* 1982, 1987).

Facing the facts

Up until the late 1970s most long-term care places for older people were provided in public sector residential care homes under the management of local authority social services departments (see Table 2.1).[1] While voluntary and, to a lesser extent, private sector provision already provided up to a third of all residential places, it was common for residential care to be seen as synonymous with the Part III home.[2] The nursing home sector at that time was small in scale and provided by the voluntary and private sectors. But, as we

Table 2.1 Nursing, residential and long-stay hospital care of elderly, chronically ill and physically disabled people: places by sector, UK, 1970–94

Year	Residential home places[1]			Nursing home places[2]		Long-stay geriatric places NHS	Long-stay psycho-geriatric places NHS	Total places
	LA	Private	Vol.	Private/Vol.				
1970	108,700	23,700	40,100	20,300		52,000	23,000	247,300
1975	128,300	25,800	41,000	24,000		49,000		
1980	134,500	37,400	42,600	26,900		46,100		
1981	135,600	40,200	44,500	26,900		46,400		
1982	136,200	46,900	44,400	27,200		46,300		
1983	136,500	54,700	45,300	29,000		46,900		
1984	137,200	67,100	45,900	32,500		46,500		
1985	137,100	85,300	45,100	38,000		46,300		
1986	136,900	99,500	46,600	47,900		45,600		
				Private	Vol.			
1987	135,500	114,600	42,200	52,000	8,300	43,000		
1988	133,500	127,900	43,000	68,700	9,600	61,400[3]	29,300	436,500
1989	129,800	143,200	39,900	88,600	10,400	49,500[4]	28,200	463,900
1990	125,600	155,600	40,000	112,600	10,500	47,200[4]	27,000	494,000
1991	117,400	161,200	41,900	135,200	12,100	44,400[4]	24,500	514,600
1992	105,200	162,400	46,900	152,800	13,700	40,200[4]	23,500	524,500
1993	95,000	165,400	51,000	168,200	15,000	37,800[4]	22,300	534,600
1994	86,400	167,500	50,700	178,800	16,000	34,700[4]	20,100	536,200

1 Includes residential places in dual registration homes; excludes 'small homes' of less than four beds, estimated at some 5,000 for the elderly and physically handicapped client group at April 1994.

2 Includes nursing places in dual registration homes.

3 The increase in 1988 is an artefact caused by reclassification of hospital types when Korner aggregates were introduced.

4 NHS long-stay geriatric beds estimated since 1988 on the assumption that acute/rehabilitation geriatric beds in England have remained constant and all the decline in beds in the speciality overall is attributable to loss of long-stay beds.

Source: adapted from Laing (1995: A191, Table 5.2).

can see from Table 2.1, the pattern of provision was to change significantly. During the 1980s, the private residential sector grew exponentially. Across this period, annual percentage increases in the number of places ranged from 17 per cent (between 1981 and 1982) to 27 per cent (between 1984 and 1985); a levelling out started in 1988, with only a 12 per cent increase between 1988 and 1989. At the same time, the voluntary sector saw small fluctuations in growth while local authority provision levelled out in 1984 and then declined. However, taken together, provision during the 1980s overtook demand as predicted by demographic change (Higgs and Victor 1993; Laing 1995).

In 1991 residential sector growth peaked, and since then there has been a small *decrease* in overall provision of the order of 1–2 per cent per annum. However, the private residential sector continued to *increase* at around 1–2 per cent per annum. In addition, figures are now available for small residential homes for fewer than four residents. These establishments numbered 5,500 in 1995, accommodating 10,300 residents, of whom 3,400 were older people.[3] Adding to the complexity of this picture, a small percentage of all residential and nursing homes are dually registered, that is, they are registered under the Registered Homes Act 1984 as providing a specified number of both residential and nursing places – 4.5 per cent in 1994 in residential settings (Laing 1995: A193, Table 5.3).

In contrast to the residential sector, the nursing home sector has seen a gradual increase throughout the 1980s and 1990s with particularly marked growth since 1985–6, especially within the private sector. In 1985, the ratio of residential to nursing home places stood at 7 to 1; by 1990 this had become 3 to 1 and, by 1994, 1.5 to 1. The changing fortunes of the nursing home sector stand in sharp relief to the steady decline in NHS long-stay beds (see Table 2.1), particularly since 1989.

What explanations have been given for these dramatic changes? As Figure 2.1 shows, a number of factors are implicated in stimulating the changes in long-term care. The most commonly quoted factor is the changing demography within the ageing population, and the increase in the numbers of people over 80 years of age. This is the group from whom the institutional population is drawn. As we shall see below, a range of factors affect people's admission to residential care, but the relationship between advanced age and increased morbidity is obviously important, and in recent years the more explicit recognition of the difficulties of caring for older people with dementia at home will have legitimated some admissions. Arguably, however, the ageing of the population may serve as a smokescreen. Importantly, it is not the determinant of the type of provision provided, even though, as Laing (1995: A118) comments, institutional living is a common experience for many people in their eighties:

> Latest (1994) figures indicate that 1 per cent of the 65–74 year old population live in some form of institutional setting, whether a local authority old people's home, an NHS hospital or a private or voluntary residential or nursing home. For people aged 85 and over, the proportion is estimated to reach 26 per cent.

Other factors are said to have a bearing on long-term care provision. These include the changing nature of family life and the place of older people in family structures, along with consumer demand. Concern has been voiced that changes in family life consequent on women's employment, women's expectations and the increase in divorce and remarriage (McGlone 1992, 1993; Kellaher *et al.* 1988) may affect the ability and willingness of family members to care for older people. However, to date there appears to be little evidence to support this view. Grundy (1992a), in a reanalysis of the 1985 General Household Survey of carers, finds that people who have been divorced are no less likely to care for older parents or parents-in-law than others, and this view is supported by preliminary findings from a more recent

Figure 2.1 Factors which may affect the demand for long-term care

---

- Demographic: increase in the number of very old people; increased morbidity with increasing age; in particular, increase in numbers of older people suffering from dementing illnesses.
- Social: changes in the pattern of family structures and responsibilities at work and at home; increased tendency for some families to live at a distance from each other.
- Economic/consumer: improved financial position of many older people; older people making a positive choice over long-term care.
- Service: increased pressure on long-stay hospital beds; more effective use of acute hospital beds; closure of psychiatric hospitals.
- Political: initial stimulation through public funding of private and voluntary provision via supplementary benefit; community care legislation; attack on residential provision. Transfer of state funding to cash-limited local authority budgets since April 1993.
- Ideological: increasing popular support for a pluralist approach to welfare during the 1980s. Increasing reliance during the late 1980s and 1990s on the market within health and social welfare services.

---

qualitative study of the impact of family change on the lives of older people (Bornat *et al.*, forthcoming). Greater longevity may, however, have an impact on the support networks available to people in their eighties and these patterns may vary for different groups and cohorts.

The suggestion that older people are 'voting with their feet' and entering residential and nursing home care at will proves very difficult to quantify. As we shall see throughout this book, the characteristics and circumstances of potential residents may in themselves be limiting, and the opportunities afforded for making real choices over accommodation and care appear to be constrained. While it is true that many older people have used public funds as well as their own resources to fund long-term care, this is very different from predicting a positive demand for places. Some older people will have lost control of their finances to other family members (Allen *et al.* 1992), and our knowledge concerning privately funded residents remains sparse.

What we do know is that the older population is diverse in terms of financial resources, ranging from those who have benefited, and who are beginning to benefit, from occupational pensions, to those who rely solely on the ever diminishing purchasing power of the state pension (Johnson 1992; Groves 1995). Evidence that the former are more likely to be men in their sixties and seventies, and, to a lesser degree, the latter are more likely to be women in their seventies and eighties, is also an important factor to take into account. Here we see the structural root of a division which has important consequences for choice and access to accommodation and care in later life.

The more tangible factors affecting changes in the development of long-term care have been those generated through ideology and policy. Since the late 1970s, the ideological support of successive Conservative governments for a market economy within health and social care has radically altered the shape and ownership of provision. Within residential care, this change can be dated back to the introduction of the Supplementary Benefits (Requirements) Regulations in 1980 which enabled people entering private residential care to obtain financial support through board and lodgings payments. This action enabled many older people on low incomes (i.e. those who qualified for income support) to enter private and voluntary sector homes by using public funds (Challis and Bartlett 1988). Moreover, this support was channelled, for the first time, through the benefits system, without any requirement for the care needs of individuals to be assessed by the local authority. It is not, perhaps, surprising that the passage of this ruling corresponds with the enormous growth already described. It was this growth which led to the subsequent spiralling of the social security bill as payments increased from £6 million in 1978 to £200 million in 1984 (Social Policy Research Unit (SPRU) 1987), and to more than £2,500 million immediately prior to the introduction of the community care reforms in 1993 (Laing 1993; Wistow 1995: 228). Seen as a 'perverse incentive' towards institutional care, this trend was central to the great debate of the late 1980s around the further development of community care (Audit Commission 1986).

The enactment of the NHS and Community Care Act 1990 and the White Papers, *Caring for People* (Department of Health 1989a) and *The Health of the Nation* (DoH 1992), presaged major changes in the management of long-term care into the foreseeable future. Thus, since April 1993, local authorities have taken over responsibility for the assessment and placement of older people funded by public moneys within residential care and nursing homes. The moneys available for such support currently come from the DSS transfer element of the Special Transitional Grant (STG) introduced during the phasing in of the new community care legislation and available to local authorities from 1993–4 to 1996–7 (see Laing 1995: A202). Eighty-five per cent of this money has been ring-fenced for spending on independent sector services, either residential or non-residential, though, to date, the sector has a greater stake in collective service provision than in domiciliary care services.

At the same time as these changes have been taking place, the NHS has also been undergoing substantial reform (Wistow 1995), and since 1989 we have seen a gradual decline in the number of long-stay geriatric and psychogeriatric hospital places (Table 2.1). Between 1989 and 1994 there was a decrease of almost 30 per cent in long-stay geriatric and psychogeriatric places. In a parallel development, this period was also characterized by the rise in the number of nursing home places. As a result of the closure of long-stay hospital provision and the transfer of older people to nursing home care, there has been a debate about the responsibilities and resource implications, with some health authorities passing on the financial responsibility for funding nursing care to local authorities. This led to the Department of Health issuing a clarification of the roles and responsibilities of health and local authorities (DoH 1995a) and, as of April 1996, both the latter authorities should have in place an agreed joint policy for the provision of people requiring continuing nursing care (DoH 1996).

Becoming an industry

These trends show that the private sector has come to dominate both residential and nursing home care and that providing care in these settings is now an industry which Laing (1995: A190) estimates is worth £8.0 billion, the private sector share of this amounting to £4.6 billion. In response to this development, the state has put in place a system of regulation aimed at setting standards of care through registration and inspection, a system which is codified in the Registered Homes Act 1984 and its accompanying regulations. Originally focused on the independent sector, such regulation has been developed and extended, through the introduction of arm's-length inspection units, and now covers all sectors of provision, both residential and domiciliary (DoH 1989a). The impact of regulation has been both subtle and extensive, and is discussed under several headings in this book.

Within the private residential care homes sector, the traditional small business entrepreneur continues to be a major provider, accounting for 40 per cent of newly registered beds in the year to mid-1994 (Laing 1995: A222). The most typical forms of provision continue to be those with husband and wife teams acting as owner-managers of only one home, or a matron-manager running a home owned by a number of local entrepreneurs. These small businesses usually occupy former domestic housing and often have a modern extension attached (Weaver *et al.* 1985). Laing (1995: A222) reports that 'the average new private (non-corporate) residential registration was 16 beds in the year to mid-1994 [whereas] the average new nursing home registration was 36 beds'.

The emphasis placed, through regulation, on the development of high-quality environments is to some degree reflected in the size of facility and is one of the explanations given for the relative lack of small business expansion within the nursing home sector. In contrast, corporate providers who have made some in-roads into the residential care sector have, in recent years, achieved control of almost a third of the for-profit nursing home sector.[4] There is some concern that, as more corporate providers enter the care industry, facilities will grow in size and the professed aim of providing a 'homely environment in the local community' (DoH 1989a: paras 1–8) will disappear:

> The goal of sustaining a cottage industry providing a network of small, high quality, local homes may prove elusive, with many fearing that the market will become dominated by large corporate providers, without local roots, providing 50–150 places, or more. Thus budgetary pressures may result in local authorities having little option but to purchase care from the kinds of large-scale institutions that they have striven to close over 30 years.
>
> (Wistow 1995: 231)

As Table 2.1 showed, the voluntary or 'not-for-profit' sector has remained relatively static throughout this period of development. However, an increase was seen during the early 1990s as many local authorities transferred their own Part III accommodation to local 'not-for-profit' trusts. The transfer of local authority provision to trust status is currently seen as a way of enabling easier access to capital investment for refurbishment, and of opening up resident access to the Residential Care Allowance which is available to individuals placed in private or voluntary homes (Laing 1995: A222). The voluntary sector, however, does have a number of large-scale providers and Laing (1995) places Anchor Housing Association alongside two or three of the large for-profit providers as an organization which now has one of the largest number of registered residential and nursing home places through the development of its 'housing with care' and 'housing with nursing care' schemes.

This discussion of providers and provision highlights the fact that, for many, long-term care has assumed the character of a business. But, of course, it is also a business with both regional and local variations. Several authors have considered the geography of residential provision (Larder *et al.* 1986; Peace 1987; Hamnett and Mullings 1992; Smith 1992), showing how in the early 1980s private and voluntary sector development was more rapid in the south of Britain (particularly in areas such as Devon, Clwyd, East and West Sussex) while public sector provision remained dominant in the north. Such a distribution developed for demographic, ideological and financial reasons, but over time there has been greater equalization in the spread of independent sector care, and, as we have noted above, changes to trust status for former local authority provision also affect the distribution.

Inevitably, those 'in the business' have a vested interest in keeping it going. The era of rapid growth has come to an end and major changes in the funding arrangements of residential and nursing home care consequent upon the community care legislation might therefore be expected to bring about radical change to this industry. Yet, to date, the evidence of a significant move away from this type of provision does not emerge very strongly. The industry's worries of beds lying empty and homes being closed has not materialized to any great extent. Laing (1995: A197) seems optimistic: 'the independent care home sector seems to have achieved a softer landing, some two years after the community care reforms, than many had predicted'. He shows that in 1994 around 90 per cent of available beds in all sectors were occupied and that, while the demand for residential care places fell slightly, as we have seen, the demand for private nursing home places increased (Laing 1995: A197, A202). Figures from the Government Statistical Service for residential care homes demonstrate that the occupancy rate remained constant at 88 per cent between 1994 and 1995 (DoH 1995d: 3). On the basis of demographic trends, Laing (1995: A197) estimates a continuing demand of around 12,000 long-term care places per annum.

Sources of finance

At present individuals may fund a place in a residential home in one of three ways: entirely through means-tested public finance; through a combination of means-tested public finance and private top-up money; and entirely through private means. Those people who were in receipt of Income Support in independent residential and nursing homes before April 1993 have had their entitlement to this benefit protected (i.e. have preserved rights) at rates which are set annually by the Department of Social Security. From April 1996 these rates were set at a limit of £203 per week for the standard rate in residential homes and £234 for very dependent older people, and at £303 per week for nursing homes. This group with preserved rights receives support at a higher rate than those who have been supported through public moneys since April 1993, although new entrants are now entitled to claim ordinary Income Support payments and a Residential Care Allowance from the Department of Social Security (DSS), both of which are subject to means testing.

Up until November 1995, individuals were not entitled to receive public funding until their assets fell below £8,000. However, measures announced in the autumn 1995 Budget, which came into effect from April 1996, raised this amount to £16,000. The lower limit, below which people do not have to contribute at all, was also raised from £3,000 to £10,000. This was a response to the general concern that increasing numbers of older people are having to utilize the capital from their property in order to pay for long-term care and that this may lead to a decline in inheritance between the generations. This effect was seen to contradict the Conservative government policy of encouraging a 'home-owning democracy'.

Of course, access to resources influences the type of care that can be purchased. To date, the annual rates for income support set by the DSS for those with preserved rights have also been used as fee benchmarks by local authorities, although there is some regional variation in these figures (Laing 1995). However, where an older person is publicly financed, the local authority must also abide by regulations which allow for individual preference provided:

- the accommodation is suitable in relation to the individual's assessed needs;
- to do so would not cost the authority more than it would usually pay for someone with the individual's assessed needs;
- the person in charge of the accommodation is willing to provide accommodation subject to the authority's usual terms and conditions.

(Laing 1995: A206)

Marrying the wishes of individuals with the contracting and bargaining which must go on between local authorities and local providers is an ongoing process which is only now becoming clear (see Laing 1995). There has always been provision for individuals and their families to choose a more expensive care home and to 'top up' fees. Laing (1995) reports that this practice is now becoming less common among local authority funded residents than among those whose arrangements were organized directly through income support. At present, the system of funding is in flux, with the different systems running in parallel. As of February 1994, 51 per cent of residents in private and voluntary nursing and residential homes were financed either wholly or partly through income support, with 28 per cent self financed; 18 per cent were now financed by the local authority and a further 3 per cent through NHS funding.

Types of environment

Table 2.2 shows the distribution of residential care homes by average number of places and sector, confirming that at present the picture of private

Table 2.2   Places in residential care homes, by type of room and sector, England, 31 March 1995

	Places in			
	Average number of places	*Single rooms (%)*	*Double rooms (%)*	*Multi rooms (%)*
All sectors	20	74	25	1
Local authority	30	83	17	0
Voluntary	19	83	15	2
Private	18	67	32	1

Source: Department of Health (1995d: 3).

residential care homes is still small-scale, generally in ordinary domestic housing. This contrasts with the larger scale of much (predominantly 1960s purpose-built) local authority provision and indicates that Wistow's fears about scale are yet to be realized. Our earlier 1980–1 data showed that the overall size of a home was important for the individual's comprehension of a building. However, we were equally – if not more – concerned with the amount of private space offered to individuals within the home and the degree of privacy afforded (Willcocks *et al.* 1987). Table 2.2 also shows that the private sector, with smaller overall numbers of places per home, continues to have a greater proportion of shared rooms. Therefore, there is an obvious tension between using an adapted house, with the constraints of space and manoeuvrability for residents but with compensatory attractive features, or a new building with enough well-designed space, for a residential home.

The figures for single-room provision given in Table 2.2 are confirmed by market surveys carried out by Laing (1995) and outlined in Table 2.3. In the nursing home sector the growth of single rooms is marked, although single rooms still form a smaller percentage than in residential homes. However, while the trend is accelerating in the nursing sector, it may have peaked in the residential sector at around two-thirds of places. The trends in the provision of en-suite toilets in the two settings reflect the changes to single rooms. Table 2.3 also shows a range of amenities, and Laing (1995: A226) comments that the private nursing and residential sectors may not be providing hotel accommodation but are certainly enhancing the range of services.

Since the mid-1980s, those involved in the design of accommodation (both exterior and interior) for older people have learnt much about those aspects of design which may enhance or support the lives of residents, as well as those features which people simply prefer (Willcocks *et al.* 1987). This has been especially true in the area of provision for older people with dementia (Marshall 1993; Dunlop 1994). Our earlier analysis of the balance of public to private space and the shifts which were starting to emerge in the mid-1980s (Willcocks *et al.* 1987) is supported by the trends in Table 2.3, which show that individual life-style is now more likely to be protected and supported by

Table 2.3   Facilities and amenities in private care homes, mid-1989 to November 1994 (per cent)

	Nursing						Residential					
	Nov '94	Jan '94	1992	1991	1990	1989	Nov '94	Jan '94	1992	1991	1990	1989
Single beds	58	57	51	49	47	44	67	66	65	63	62	60
Beds with en-suite toilet	27	23	24	22	18	17	28	26	27	26	22	22
Homes offering care for elderly severely mentally ill (supervised by registered mental nurse)	19	18	19	18	18	15	0	0	0	0	0	0
Homes offering respite care	81	81	73	69	67	52	72	68	60	48	49	35
Homes offering day care	21	19	16	17	16	11	32	28	27	22	21	16
Homes offering home care	11	12	7	8	10	na	15	17	17	18	20	na
Homes offering terminal care	70	73	74	73	75	70	24	26	26	27	26	27
Homes offering consultant-supervised post-operative/ convalescent care	18	21	19	24	26	29	0	0	0	0	0	0
Homes offering hydrotherapy	3	5	4	4	5	5	1	2	2	1	2	3
Homes with bar/café	4	4	5	4	4	4	3	3	4	3	4	5
Homes with minibus	24	26	23	22	22	20	23	21	21	19	20	22
Homes with separate activities room	24	24	26	25	27	22	18	16	19	19	20	21

Source: Laing (1995: A206).

more creative design of private and public space within residential homes. Where older people who have cognitive impairments are concerned, attention has been given to the design of residential and nursing settings with the aim of enhancing control over the environment (Lawton 1980). However, all advances in design will have cost implications. Many homes operate within the limitations of the original building and restrict any upgrade to the minimal regulatory requirements. We return to issues concerning the form and function of residential care homes in Chapter 5 and the impact of regulation in Chapter 6.

Characteristics of residents

In Willcocks *et al.* (1987) we considered Townsend's (1962: 59) view that older people living in residential homes were 'markedly different' from those living in the community. Our study in 1980–1(Willcocks *et al.* 1982) focused on local authority residential homes, and we analysed data based on 1,000 residents in 100 homes. At that time, the average ages for residents were 83 years for women and 79 years for men, with 82 per cent of the sample over the age of 75 years. Thus the residential world was, and remains, dominated by the very old. Through comparison with census data and the creation of a profile for a typical 40-bed home, we learnt a number of things about the basic characteristics of residents (see Willcocks *et al.* 1987: 35, Figure 2 and Table 1). For example, women over 85 years of age were overrepresented in the residential population. Among younger residents (60–75 years) a large percentage were divorced, separated, or never married, with rates much higher than the general population, and this was particularly true of male residents; it was also the case among men over 75 years. The percentage of widowed male residents was again much higher than for men of a similar age living in the community, reflecting the level of spouse support which normally prevails between older people.

Almost half of our 1980–1 sample had been living alone prior to entering residential care, and while this was not unusual for older women, given sex differences in mortality and age differences between married people, the men were disproportionately living alone prior to entry when compared to census data. In addition, there was evidence that, over time, more residential places were being occupied by those who had previously lived alone than by those who had lived with others. Another important factor in terms of living arrangements was that a significant proportion of residents had been living in another institutional setting – a hospital or another residential home – before being admitted to their residential home.

These findings, though 15 years old, have a familiar ring to them and have been supported by a number of authors writing more recently (Sinclair 1988; Arber and Ginn 1990; Higgs and Victor 1993). Thus the residential world and the world of long-term care are still characterized by very old women, with marital status and living arrangements being important factors for becoming a resident (see Grundy 1992a: 71). In addition, Sinclair (1988: 255) showed that, while the numbers of older people with high levels of disability was, and continues to be, higher in the community, a much higher proportion of those living in residential care have increased levels of incapacity, and research suggests that maintaining older people in the community is more difficult if they are suffering from mental incapacity such as dementia than from a physical incapacity (Sinclair 1988: 258). These findings are confirmed by more recent evidence from the OPCS survey of disabled adults (see Higgs and Victor 1993) and the 1991 census, with women, particularly those over 85 years, living in a range of communal settings being more likely to have a long-term illness than their counterparts in the community.

But while these data tell us that mental or physical incapacity are obviously important factors, they are not the sole reasons for admission. Older people are less likely to enter residential care if a number of conditions are present:

- if they have informal support in the community and if that support can be maintained;
- if their income is sufficient to maintain or enhance that support at home and delay a move to residential care;
- if socio-economic status is higher rather than lower;
- if their housing environment is conducive to coping with levels of disability;
- if their lack of resources is compensated for by community services

(see Weaver *et al.* 1985; Grundy 1992a; Higgs and Victor 1993). The importance of this combination of factors is evident in this quote from our earlier study:

Our analysis shows that there is some evidence of selection bias amongst residents, but that this is particularly true of younger residents and male residents. The characteristics of 'very' old women, who form a majority of residents, are similar to old women living in the community. This group, rather than being perceived as deviant, may simply be those who have survived beyond the limits of their community support. All of these factors point to the importance of social circumstances in influencing admissions, and support the suggestion that the old person newly admitted to residential care may be characterised by one or more of the following features: aged over seventy-five years, single, childless, living alone.

(Willcocks *et al.* 1987: 36–7)

We still know relatively little about the ethnic characteristics of residents in residential settings and whether race and culture are important factors in determining accommodation and care in later life. Research from the USA indicates that higher rates of residential living occur among whites (see Grundy 1992a), and this appears to be true in Britain, given the small percentages of older people from the various minority ethnic groups resident in communal establishments on the night of the 1991 census (OPCS and General Register Office for Scotland 1993). In Britain members of minority ethnic groups make up a small percentage of the population over 65 years, and a recent postal survey of 412 residential and nursing homes revealed only 1 per cent of residents from minority ethnic groups (Katz *et al.* 1996). The need for accommodation and care can be very community-specific and, to date, sheltered housing and residential care tailored to local needs has been the preferred solution for people from minority ethnic groups (NISW 1993; Blakemore and Boneham 1994; Jones 1994). The characteristics of these schemes have facilitated the preservation of cultural mores and the personal integrity of individuals and groups whose life-style is distinctive and different from that of the white majority. They may also offer a degree of protection from the hostility and/or racism which old people from minority ethnic groups may experience and enable this experience to be addressed within the philosophy of care (see NISW 1993: Chapter 6). Evidence suggests that many residential care services fail to acknowledge and respond positively to cultural difference (Patel 1990). Hence, residential care may be rejected in order to minimize the effect described by Norman (1985) as 'triple jeopardy'.

In a more recent study Opit and Pahl (1993) attempted to predict some of the characteristics of those people most likely to be admitted to institutional care, with the aim of developing a model for use by those trying to plan for such provision within their locality. Again, utilizing the OPCS Disability Survey from 1988, they considered the characteristics of those respondents who, while sampled for the study, either died or were admitted to an institution before interview. For those at risk of admission, key variables were the degree of care needed – with short interval care (three to four times a day to almost continual care) being most important – along with living alone and the presence of dementia. In analysing the interaction between these factors they found that while those people living alone were less disabled than those living with others, 'for any given state of disability, living alone increases the risk of admission three-fold'. They were also able to show that among those entering institutional care '33 per cent are likely to suffer from severe cognitive disability, and 39 per cent from severe incontinence, while 27 per cent will be relatively immobile' (Opit and Pahl 1993: 5) and that these conditions may be more prevalent among those who have previously been living with other people.

Staff in homes

Many attempts have been made to encapsulate in a simple model the normal staffing arrangements expected in residential and nursing establishments. According to one authority:

> A typical 35-bedded nursing home should have two trained nurses plus five care assistants and, in many cases, a supernumerary matron and a range of ancillary staff to carry out domestic duties. This can be compared to a typical 35-bed residential home, which would have two care assistants and a senior care assistant on an early shift. The senior care assistant will be expected to undertake some administrative duties and the care assistants will usually have domestic and laundry duties, in addition to the provision of client care.
>
> (O'Kell 1995: 15)

Staff in residential homes can be categorized under a number of headings: care staff, managerial staff, supervisory staff; domestic staff; ancillary staff; and visiting professionals. The main work in looking after the needs of residents falls to the care staff, both day and night, and they form the largest group. The size of the care staff group within any one home can vary and is very much dependent on the underlying aims and objectives of the home and how these are put into practice. If the aim is to provide a person-centred approach to care, where the needs of the residents as individuals and as a group are taken as a starting point for developing staff duties, then the formation of this staff group may be very different from one where the staff rota dictates the type of care available. This balancing act between the needs of residents and of staff is not easy but in *Home Life* (Centre for Policy on Ageing 1984) and its sequel, *A Better Home Life* (CPA, 1996) and in *Residential Care: Positive Answers* (NISW 1993) what is stressed is the range of care work, the peaks and troughs of needs, and the changing characteristics of residents:

> There is no absolutely correct staffing for each unit, but various factors need to be borne in mind in coming to a decision. The amount of physical work to be done, the need for individual attention, peaks in demand, the likelihood of control problems, additional duties such as escorting of individuals outside the home all need to be considered. It is also essential to maintain a degree of flexibility to cover the unforeseen difficulties which inevitably crop up in residential work, and which make the job demanding and fascinating.
>
> (NISW 1993: 93)

In *A Better Home Life* mechanistic staff–resident ratios are not recommended, although *Home Life* did offer some basic guidance on how staff cover could be determined:

> As a rule of thumb, with allowance made for time off, holidays and some illness, a home needs to employ 3.5 staff to provide one person on day duty. Where at least two staff are needed on duty at all times, the minimum cover would therefore demand $3.5 \times 2 = 7.00$ staff. These figures are given in full-time equivalents, but could be filled by part-time staff, or a mixture of full- and part-timers.
>
> (CPA 1984: 51)

The Wagner group of experts, looking at staffing arrangements, recognized that resident group had changed over the years; people were now physically and mentally frailer, and it was argued that this needed to be recognized in terms of roles and skills changes within staffing.

> In some homes for older people, staffing levels still relate to a time when residents were generally fitter and more lucid; greater clarity about the target group of residents would reveal the creeping change towards increased confusion and frailty, and the need to adapt staffing arrangements.
>
> (NISW 1993: 90)

While the regulations regarding nursing homes stipulate the number of staff who should have nursing qualifications, in residential homes the most important factors are that staff should have the 'right skills, knowledge and experience in the right volume to match the scale of residents' needs' (NISW 1993: 92).

At the time of our earlier studies in local authority and private residential homes (Willcocks *et al.* 1982; 1987; Weaver *et al.* 1985) care staff were characteristically young or middle-aged women who worked part-time. The former group were typically those who had failed in earlier career aspirations and had 'arrived' in residential care work as a last option; the latter group were often a return-to-work group, fulfilling multiple roles in the family and in the workplace. Neither group would generally be qualified, nor would they have high expectations with regard to on-the-job training. There were few male members of care staff. In contrast, the majority of supervisory and managerial staff were men and women who worked full-time. This pattern still prevails. A recent study of local authority social services staff carried out by the NISW Research Unit (Balloch *et al.* 1995) showed that residential workers, particularly with older people, were predominantly women who were often older than other social services staff. There was also a high representation of black workers among residential staff. National figures for staff working in the independent sector are not available.

The range of tasks undertaken by care staff is varied and, though frequently dominated by the physical care of residents, can also include social and health care, domestic/cleaning tasks, rehabilitative and palliative care, and in some cases, administration. Much depends on the way staff are managed: whether separate domestic staff are employed; whether care staff have specific key worker roles; whether the home operates some form of small-group living which involves specific group work. Variations in ways of working are also seen among supervisory staff who may be more or less involved in domestic bursar/housekeeping functions. In some cases these duties are split so that senior staff may devote more time to resident and staffing issues – for example, having an oversight of staff training. These variations in role can be seen in the current job advertisements for residential staff given below (see Figure 2.2). They are also reflected in the salaries offered: in spite of the variation, these remain relatively low for senior staff and very low for care staff, with an hourly rate in 1996 which may range between £2.50 and £4.50 in different parts of Britain.

This brings us to the key issues of staff support, supervision and training, seen by all commentators as the basis of good practice (CPA 1984; 1996; NISW 1993). We have already noted that, with the exception of qualified nursing staff in nursing homes, qualifications are not legally required for those managing and working in residential homes, although the test of 'fit person' carried out by registering authorities may well take account of the qualifications of owners and managers. We also see in job advertisements that senior staff are often expected to have a social work qualification.

But the training of care staff is more problematic. Again, the NISW research shows that among residential workers surveyed in a study of social services staff, two-fifths had some educational qualifications, and although they were the most motivated group in terms of wanting qualifications, they also had the least access to training (Balloch *et al.* 1995). Trained staff are now being seen as an important indicator of quality by those who contract for care places and those who register and inspect homes. Thus, the emphasis has been placed upon induction training, ongoing in-house training and the emergent National Vocational Qualification (S/NVQ) in Care, which compare levels of performance against the special requirements of the job (NISW 1990; 1993; O'Kell 1995).

However, training is also costly, both in time and in resources; hence, the type of training provided needs to maximize both. To date, figures are not

Figure 2.2   Typical job advertisements

SERVICE MANAGER, Elderly Persons' Home   £21,651

A permanent vacancy exists at Lemon Tree EPH. Desborough MBC provides a quality residential service to elderly people who are assessed via the care management system as being unable to live independently in the community.

You will be a member of an experienced group of managers committed to promoting and developing services for older people and their carers in Desborough. You should have a minimum of two years' experience at a senior level in residential care and possess a relevant qualification (i.e. CQSW, DipSW, CSS). Applications will also be considered from senior members of staff who do not have the recognised qualifications, but who have acted in the capacity of Manager for a continuous period of at least six months. You will need to demonstrate:

- commitment to good practice incorporating resident choice and participation;
- an ability to manage budgets;
- skills in leading and motivating staff;
- knowledge of relevant legislation;
- effective communication skills.

CARE ASSISTANTS

We are a 30 bedded residential home in the London Borough of Westwood, caring for physically frail older people. We are looking for highly motivated Care Assistants who wish to join our caring, hardworking team, committed to providing a high standard of care.

We need day staff – 20/39 hours per week at £4.39 per hour plus w/end enhancement and also night staff – 33/34 hours per week at £4.63 per hour plus w/end enhancement.

We are looking for people who: understand the needs of older people, are honest and friendly, kind and considerate, flexible and reliable, and able to communicate well with people.

We are working to achieve BS5750 and are working towards Investors in People. Our homes have regular training programmes and NVQ training at Level II will be available to suitable candidates.

---

available concerning how many residential care workers have undertaken the S/NVQ in Care at levels 2 or 3. Views on the most appropriate system for training are mixed (NISW 1993; O'Kell 1995), although findings from a study by the Joseph Rowntree Foundation (1994) suggested that staff trained through the S/NVQ system were more responsive to clients' needs and required less direct supervision. The study went on to argue that the S/NVQ programme encouraged a greater appreciation of the underlying values of clients' rights, choice and control, and offered a way of developing multi-skilled staff bridging the gap between nursing and care staff. The last issue of multi-skilling is becoming particularly important as more care staff are called upon to undertake 'nursing care' and as registering authorities are considering the range of tasks which may be delegated by a community nurse to care staff (O'Kell 1995: 18).

Residential homes today and yesterday

We can see from the discussion so far that since the early 1980s, while much of the fabric of residential life has remained the same, there have been a number of changes, not only within the homes – among residents and staff – but also in how they are financed and supported. Figure 2.3 presents three case studies which highlight some of the similarities and differences we have been describing.

An examination of these perspectives and our prior discussion reminds us of a number of areas where residential care has changed or remained the same.

Figure 2.3   Residential changes over time: three case studies

Reppon Lodge, 1982

Built in the late 1960s, Reppon Lodge is a two-storeyed, L-shaped, purpose-built home for 40 residents, run by a local authority. The two wings have respective daytime and night-time roles, the one being predominantly bedroom space, and the other containing lounge space, the dining room, office space and storage. Half of the residents share bedrooms. There are communal bathrooms and WCs and no en-suite facilities.

The home serves a generally rural community, and some of the residents have moved into the home from adjacent sheltered housing. The residents are mostly women, with an average age of 81 years for the whole group.

The staff are nearly all middle-aged women, living locally, none of whom has received any formal training. 'Sitting with Nelly' is the norm. The male officer in charge is assisted by his wife, who has been appointed as deputy. They and another couple, who are assistant managers, all live in on-site accommodation.

Bargate House, 1987

A privately owned home for 26 older people, Bargate House has been running as an old people's home for 20 years. It is in a seaside location. The owners originally opened a home for 16 residents in a converted hotel. After 10 years, the owner and his wife, who is a qualified nurse, decided to expand. They have had a modern extension built which has added a further ten bedrooms, seven of which have en-suite facilities, and an additional dining area. Throughout this expansion the domestic (care and cleaning) staff has increased; a senior care officer has been appointed, and a deputy manager has taken over administrative and community liaison work.

The home is registered with the local authority and has witnessed the recent development of the registration and inspection system under the Registered Homes Act. A majority of the residents pay privately, and the current fees are £190 per week.

The Willows, 1995

The Willows is a home for 40 people run by a not-for-profit trust which has been contracted by the local authority to provide 20 places for its funded residents. The remaining residents are self-supported. It was formerly a local authority home and was built in the early 1970s along group-living lines. The design features five units for eight residents, with six single rooms and one shared room in each unit. The units stand around a common central courtyard. Some major refurbishment is needed to the outside of the building, and it is hoped that work will commence this year.

There are presently 35 women and 5 men resident, and one unit is used by older people with dementia. The home is run by the manager and her deputy. There are 2 senior care assistants and 10 care assistants, some part-time and some full-time. The staff–resident ratio fluctuates throughout the day, but during the early shift it is 1:10. Four members of the care staff are undertaking the S/NVQ in Care at level 2 and one at level 3. The home is also carrying out its own quality assurance programme and has implemented a complaints system. Both staff training and quality assurance are areas which have been discussed with the registration officer who now inspects the home at least twice a year, excluding occasional unannounced visits.

- Residents in all three homes are predominantly older women.
- Care staff remain predominantly female and poorly paid.
- Training remains an expensive entity and tends to be associated with higher staffing grades; but
- training for care staff is becoming increasingly important. The S/NVQ in Care has been introduced; however, homes still need to be able to afford to facilitate training.
- Regulation has been developed to cover not only the independent sector but also local authority provision.
- Some local authorities have transferred their own provision to not-for-profit trusts.
- Fewer residents are entering residential care purely for reasons of accommodation.
- The physical environment of many new homes has improved with greater privacy and service support.
- The financing of residential care has changed.
- More residents are coming into residential care with mental health problems.

Predispositions to living and working in residential settings

In Chapter 1 the history of institutional provision was discussed. In this chapter our analysis of current trends shows that, to date, a failure to develop and provide alternative forms of support for very frail older people living at home means that some groups appear to be more predisposed to a residential move than are others. For these people, choices may be (perhaps severely) constrained. In discussions of care, the relatives of residents constitute a much more visible part of the picture than was previously the case; although for them, a say in the organization of residential care has yet to be properly acknowledged. Whether as intimate carers or distant carers, many will feel guilty over the failure of themselves or their families to care for their older relative. While some may feel relief at the abdication of the caring role, others will feel at a loss, as formal carers take over, leaving them with little to do but visit (White 1994). Thus, some groups of older residents and their relatives and friends are less able to control those circumstances and events which can culminate in a residential move.

What, then, of staff? How far are they predisposed to residential care work? Women's experience as carers at home, in the absence of extensive training programmes, remains their main qualification for care work, at assistant level at least. This means that, unless there are alternatives in the local labour market, care work, poorly remunerated as it may often be, is an occupation to which large numbers of women, especially those from minority ethnic groups, and increasingly some men, are predisposed. Yet while they may also be groups with few local options for work, they can exert a powerful influence over residents. The staff group will bring to their work a mix of professional values and personal feelings about ageing, coupled with their own family experiences of older people.

The relationships developed between residents, staff and relatives will depend greatly on experiences, beliefs and attitudes. In some circumstances cultural and racial differences within and between staff and resident groups may lead to tension and conflict, and this needs to be recognized. Relationships will also be shaped by their attitudes towards the institutions in which they live, work and visit; how far they have engaged with the history and associated meanings of institutional care, and their understanding of what their residential home is trying to achieve. For staff, training may suggest to them that their role is therapeutic – one of maximizing the well-being of older people at the end of their lives. But to what extent are they equipped or encouraged to reflect upon their formal care tasks and, in the absence of such reflection, is it possible to define and enhance good practice?

Finally, while we acknowledge the potential vulnerability of older individuals to a range of influences, we should also recognize that strengths and resources need not be surrendered on moving into care. Everyone has a story to tell and many older residents are survivors, not just in terms of longevity, but also in the sense of living through immense personal and societal change. Residents and staff are individuals who will have taken on board issues of personal responsibility throughout their lives and have lived within the legal and ethical frameworks of their society. There is a richness of lived experience which underpins life in the home – both for the resident *in situ* and for the residential worker. It is to this experience of life in the home to which we now turn.

Notes

1 The term 'long-term care places' includes nursing, residential and long-stay hospital care.
2 The term 'Part III' relates to the National Assistance Act 1948 which placed a duty on local authorities to provide accommodation and care (see Chapter 1).
3 Homes with less than four places have been required to register with local authorities since 1 April 1983 under the terms of the Registered Homes (Amendment) Act 1991.
4 Laing (1995: A223) defines major corporate providers to include 'publicly quoted or foreign owned companies, BES public offers, provident associations such as PPP, private companies, individuals or partnerships with three or more homes and voluntary sector organisations with three or more homes'.

3

Life in care: Policy, practice and experience

As we have seen in Chapter 2, certain groups of older people are more likely to move into residential homes than are others, and some are more likely to have influence over this decision than others. In this chapter we are concerned with what happens to people on the threshold of residential care and beyond, as they construct their lives as residents. Again, we will draw on a number of sources: we consider the rhetoric and the realities of policy and practice, and we try to map out the residential experience for older people and their carers – both formal and informal. In particular, we consider whether the processes of residential life undermine the ability of older people to retain a good sense of identity, recognizing that at the end of life individuals will feel a need to reconcile the past and the present (Erikson 1982) and move forwards, to be in control, and, at a minimum, an active participant in the process of change.

It is the idea of residents maintaining control which runs through the principles of residential care recommended in the Wagner report (Figure 3.1). In summary, Wagner supports the idea of participating adulthood to the end of life. However, Wagner also conveys an idea of activity which may not be attractive to all residents. Later in this chapter we will return to the complex issues which surround personal autonomy, particularly at later stages in life and in collectivized settings. But we start by reviewing the research evidence on the experience of becoming a resident, alongside the principles of the Wagner report.

Becoming a resident

In his review of research for the Wagner committee in 1988, Ian Sinclair showed that among older people entering local authority residential care only a minority made a positive choice. For the majority, finding information and

Figure 3.1 Principles from *Residential Care: A Positive Choice* (NISW 1988a: 114)

> - People who move into a residential establishment should do so by positive choice. A distinction should be made between need for accommodation and need for services. No one should be required to change their permanent accommodation in order to receive services which could be made available to them in their own homes.
> - Living in a residential establishment should be a positive experience ensuring a better quality of life than the resident could enjoy in any other setting.
> - Local authorities should make efforts, as a matter of urgency, to meet the special needs of people from ethnic minority communities for residential and other services.
> - Every person who moves into a residential establishment retains their rights as a citizen. Measures need to be taken to ensure that individuals can exercise their rights. Safeguards should be applied when rights are curtailed.
> - People who move into a residential establishment should continue to have access to the full range of community support services.
> - Residents should have access to leisure, educational and other facilities offered by the local community and the right to invite and receive relatives and friends as they choose.
> - Residential staff are the major resource and should be valued as such. The importance of their contribution needs to be recognized and enhanced.

making decisions about residential care were usually tasks undertaken by someone else. Few applicants for residential care appear to have had the details they needed to make an informed choice, and many 'appear to be resigned or ambivalent about the idea of going in or to reject the idea entirely' (Sinclair 1988: 264). More recent research confirms these observations (Allen *et al.* 1992; Counsel & Care 1992a; Phillips 1992; Caldock 1994). In their study of older service users, Allen *et al.* (1992: 105) quote one man's comments on residential care: 'If I was pretty helpless then I would. If I could not walk, keep myself clean and could not feed myself'.

Such expressions of the importance of 'self-maintenance' are overwhelming. However, comments made in the abstract by older people in the community, as opposed to those made about the reality by residents, reveal the differences between 'what is wished for or expected and, on the other hand, what is achieved' (Counsel & Care 1992a). There appears to be an almost universal antipathy towards residential care which centres around the importance of maintaining the self in a particular context and setting which may compromise identity. While housing in the form of shelter, and hospital in the form of medical care, may be seen as legitimate reasons for relocating, residential care is viewed by many as not legitimate.

Decisions about entering or not entering a residential home need also to be seen in relation to the alternatives. Recent developments in community care provision and assessment of need may have led older people to hope that the choice as to whether to move into residential care or not could be made positively (DoH 1989a). But ongoing research shows that this is not the case; indeed, changes in funding arrangements for residential care and the decline in numbers of long-term care beds in hospitals have meant that decisions about residential care now depend on other factors: family finance, ownership of property, availability of informal care and support, and the local authority budget.

The process of becoming a resident may centre around a set of events which occur in quick succession, or may be traced to an accumulation of changes which gradually undermine the individual's ability to live at home (Lawrence et al. 1987; Neill et al. 1988). Willcocks et al. (1982) commented on the way in which reasons for admission to care settings may also take on legitimate or illegitimate meanings. Older people in residential care appear to have a view as to what constitutes legitimate and non-legitimate reasons for entry. For example, where an informal carer could no longer cope, then it is seen as appropriate for an older person to move into care; if the would-be carer refuses to cope, then this is seen as inappropriate or 'illegitimate'. Research shows that maintenance of a degree of influence, if not of control, over decision-making is crucial to well-being and adjustment in a residential setting (Willcocks et al. 1987; Tobin 1989; Reed and Roskell Payton 1995b). In her discussion of 'losing your home', Norman (1980: 15) comments on how this form of loss may damage the self:

> It must also be true that they are likely to work through the loss only if they make a positive identification with their new life. If they are being moved in conformity with ruling social values which are offended by letting them stay where they are, or are forced to go by the physical duress of having no viable alternative, they are still less likely to recover from the loss.

In quoting Lieberman, Norman also shows that those people who find most stressful the change of place and the adaptive process involved in relocating to residential care, may well be the very group, the most vulnerable, for which it is the only option. On the other hand, 'those who need institutional support the least are those who are most likely to survive the move into it' (Norman 1980: 16).

Studies of relocation have continued to show how cognitive ability, physical state, and aspects of personality are powerful predictors of the outcome of relocation (Norman 1980: 16). Relocation in itself, then, involves risk to self and to identity.

We have already noted that during periods of crisis or stress, older people may be especially vulnerable to the influence and actions of others. There is also research to show that if an older person moves into hospital, or has regular respite care, carers may reassess their situations (Norman 1980; Levin et al. 1989). Norman (1980: 18) describes how such reassessment may lead to a closing up of the 'social space' in which the older person has been living.

Thus, older people's personal strengths and identities may be submerged by other people's agendas.

It is also the case that changes in patterns of responsibility arising from admission to hospital may influence the behaviour of informal carers. Relatives caring at home are as circumspect about residential services as are older people, viewing them as something which could be avoided if care was shared. They too, however, are often constrained by a lack of alternatives. Allen *et al.* (1992: 106) comment:

> What did the carers think? Most of them confirmed the impressions given by the elderly people who were reluctant to consider residential care. Carers stressed the independence of the elderly people, often commenting on the fear the elderly people had of losing their autonomy.

One carer said: 'I feel very torn. I'd feel I could cope if I could get her up in the morning. It's the old story and I would feel guilty if she went' (Allen *et al.* 1992: 107).

The locus of decision-making is clearly important. While a move into hospital is unlikely to be permanent, a move from hospital to a home is very likely to herald the end of domestic living. Active participation in such decision-making while in a hospital setting is typically compromised; personal strength is at a low ebb in the face of powerful professionals, and it may not serve their interests to offer support. This situation is not uncommon. Caldock (1994), in a small-scale study with older people faced with leaving hospital, shows how inter-professional differences and conflicts of opinion can affect the types of services which become available to older people. For those faced with hospital discharge, the attitudes and knowledge of key health professionals are crucial; consultants appear to place greater emphasis on institutional solutions. Compounding this bias, many professionals fail to see the person behind the medical condition, and issues of responsibility and accountability between professionals may cloud the picture and prevent those involved from seeing how the wishes of the older person could be carried out.

In many cases, older people are perceived as being unable to manage the risks and responsibilities which follow from their decisions – for instance, to stay at home – and they are denied the right to do so. Yet decisions about moving into residential care are likely to involve some very personal trade-offs: personal care versus personal neglect; security versus privacy; company versus solitude; warmth and regular food versus familiar places and objects. Most of all, the older person has to balance which of these trade-offs is likely to support identity and well-being as a whole person. It can be argued that the trade-offs in favour of residential care are in the direction of physical/physiological maintenance; the body 'at the expense of' of mind and spirit. Perhaps this is one of the many examples where a biological model of ageing superimposes itself on sociocultural understandings. The question has to be posed: is this emphasis on the material advantages of residential care indicative of a loss of self or not? If it is, can it be changed? What is often the case, however, for many older people faced with these decisions is that they are not permitted the time to think them through. For at the time of decision-making there are other kinds of pressures (personal health, needs of other people, the physical environment to be managed), and these are likely to be very strong.

This review suggests that there is very little evidence of people positively planning a move into residential care, and yet there are examples of older people who do want to shed the risks and responsibilities of living alone in the community. Allen *et al.* (1992: 165) record this woman who viewed the conviviality offered through residential life as preferable to the changing community in which she lived:

> I just couldn't cope with it. I couldn't live at home. Those empty houses each side; they all went to work and I did not say anything to anyone. I was so lonely. Just so fed up and on my own. Here it's company.

For those most likely to be faced with residential care – the very old, the most disabled, women living alone, men without family support, people with poor mental health, those without financial resources – decision-making from a position of any power is difficult unless others appreciate the importance of the decisions, recognize the ways older people are disempowered and provide the circumstances for informed choice and the maintenance of connectedness.

Institutionalization: the evidence?

> People outside homes were unequivocal: they wished to retain as much independence as possible. They wanted to be able to go out when they chose to, not to be pushed about, and to have no restrictions. As one person said, 'freedom to be yourself: you wouldn't want to be regimented'. Close behind this in importance was the recognised need for company within a home and visits from family and friends. Thirdly, the quality of the care given by the staff was recognised as important; people wished to be treated with kindness and respect. Fourth in importance was the desire to have private space, a room of their own.
>
> (Counsel & Care 1992a: 12)[1]

These views of older people living in the community raise four of the most commonly cited aspects of residential living: regime and personal freedom; social relationships; quality of care; and the physical environment. These aspects have, for some decades now, been at the centre of discussion about quality of life in institutional care (see Willcocks *et al.* 1987; Sinclair 1988; Gibbs and Sinclair 1992). The desire of the older people studied in these texts for 'normality' stands alongside the earlier findings of Willcocks *et al.* (1982) that residents' socio-environmental choices were characterized by the wish for 'normal, unexceptional and non-institutional living'. How far is this achievable in a residential home and, given the losses incurred in the move to residential care, can earlier domestic experience be replicated in an equivalent and recognizable form? What of the view that the residential home as an institutional system itself creates dependency and stifles individual autonomy and self-determination, thus compromising personal well-being? Does residential life contribute to the process of disempowerment which people may

Figure 3.2   Values underpinning an engaged existence and the threats from institutional life

---

- **Autonomy**
  depersonalization, infantilization
- **Choice**
  rigidity of routine, structured living, resource-rich/resource-sparse environment
- **Dignity**
  block treatment of people
- **Individuality**
  residents seen as homogeneous
- **Self-determination**
  levels of staff-determined as opposed to resident-determined behaviour
- **Integration**
  social distance between staff and residents
- **Privacy**
  balance of public and private living
- **Citizenship**
  participation both within and outside the home; degree of isolation or integration with community

---

experience in the transition to a home, or does it offer an alternative, collective life-style which is simply different to domestic living and to which some people are more able to adjust than are others, at the end of their lives?

Here we review the evidence, but first we need to consider the characteristics of institutionalization, as it is commonly discussed in the literature, in relation to residential homes, and the underlying personal values which may be at risk.

As we saw in Chapter 1, many authors have sought to understand the role of institutions and the interactions of those who live and work within them (see Jones and Fowles 1984; Willcocks *et al.* 1987: 104–10). In terms of influence on British research in residential homes, Goffman's *Asylums* (1961), in particular his analysis of the characteristics of 'total institutions', remains the key text. (We shall be returning to the influence of Goffman in Part Two.) Goffman's characteristics of total institutions are as follows:

- batch living – daily life *en masse*;
- binary management – two groups (the managed and the managers);
- inmate role – losing roles, disculturation.

These aspects of the institution are outlined and elaborated in the four essays which form *Asylums*. In Figure 3.2 we utilize these characteristics in relation to commonly held underpinning values for daily living in order to highlight the relationships between them.

The evidence fuelling the institutionalization debate on residential care comes from a wealth of research, from both sides of the Atlantic, commissioned and undertaken for a variety of objectives and adopting a range of methods, from small-scale ethnographic studies to larger-scale survey research (see, for example, Gubrium 1975; Kayser-Jones 1981; Judge and Sinclair 1986; Savishinsky 1991; Peace 1993a). Methods have included structured surveys, in-depth narratives, group discussions, focus groups, participant observation and the analysis of written evidence. Few studies have been able to incorporate a longitudinal element, although where this has been achieved it has added greatly to our understanding of process (for example, Tobin and Lieberman 1976; Booth 1985). Many authors have commented on the low expectations of older people interviewed within residential settings and the difficulties they seem to experience in commenting on a home in which they will live out their lives (Hughes and Wilkin 1987; Booth 1993). To overcome some of these difficulties, researchers have stressed the value of a multimethod approach to research design (Kellaher and Peace 1990). More recently the work of Hazan (1980; 1992) and Gubrium (1993) has illuminated the value of in-depth qualitative research to our understanding of quality of life and meaning for older people now living in institutional settings.

It is not our intention to consider the findings of all this research in detail as they are discussed elsewhere (Sinclair 1988; 1990; Sinclair and Gibbs 1993; Peace 1993a). Rather, we wish to focus on that research which helps us to understand how older people seek to maintain their sense of self within residential care and how this may be eroded. While the written evidence submitted to the Wagner review of residential care in 1985–8 was weighted towards the 'positive' rather than the 'negative' (see NISW 1988a: 130) the evidence from more systematic research appears to show that although particular individuals may be happy with their circumstances and have adjusted to life in a home, for a larger proportion the potential for further disempowerment, through institutional practices, persists.

The characteristics of institutionalization outlined above imply a loss of rights and a loss of influence. This can be demonstrated where regimes operating in homes give residents little opportunity to exercise choice over the way they spend their day; how they organize use of personal time; what they eat, and when; whom they engage in conversation; and how they present in what may be experienced as an alien environment. Such a lack of influence tends to depersonalize individuals and undermine personal dignity. While this aspect of living in some residential settings has been highlighted for many years and while changes have taken place within particular settings, it is a characteristic which still pervades many homes. In delivering a service to large groups of people, the influence of the organization is relatively stronger than that of individuals and can overwhelm the capacity of residents and staff to individualize and protect key features of a personal life-style. Such imbalance needs to be constantly checked. Again, the study by Counsel & Care of the wishes and expectations of older people in the community and the lives of residents demonstrates this point:

> Most people (81 per cent) considering residential care wanted to be able to choose what time they would get up in the morning, but only 56 per

cent thought this would be possible. Of those in homes only 52 per cent had choice on this matter. In nearly a half of homes, residents still have to fit in with the regime of the home and get up when they are told. There could be no more damning statistics of the inhumanity of institutionalisation.

(Counsel & Care 1992a: 17)

Such practices are not only organizationally convenient, but also based on assumptions that residents are no longer capable of thinking for themselves, a viewpoint that is both paternalistic and infantilizing. Of course, some residents will say that they are living in residential care in order 'to be looked after' and that 'they do not want to do things for themselves'. This is an explanation which needs to be acknowledged as it reflects the rationale of residential care – that is, a place in which to care or to be cared for. The point to be made, however, is that older people have a range of needs. For staff it can be easier for the 'collective' to overshadow the 'individual' and for people to be seen as passive and accepting and as a homogeneous group needing the same kind of care.

It is also true that while attitudes such as these may be more prevalent among those working with older people, they are symptomatic, perhaps, of a wider ageism in society. This point is illustrated again in evidence from the Wagner report, where one younger physically disabled person talked of the 'philosophy of participation':

Where I was before I didn't feel that I was a human being . . . all my responsibilities were taken from me. I even went to the loo when they told me to . . . . Where I am living now I control my own life and no-one tells me what to do. One of the main things that makes the difference is the philosophy of facilitation, which means the staff are our arms and legs. It means I can control my own life.

(NISW 1988a: 148)

The commentator analysing this material does not challenge the view that older people must accept their lot, reflecting a sense of resignation:

While many of the physically handicapped appear to have the physical and intellectual energy to set about changing their situation, for the elderly and their relatives faced with a type of care they would not have chosen, acceptance sometimes appears the only route to contentment. A 90 year old sums up this position: 'I hated giving up my home but realised I couldn't go on. I've adapted'.

(NISW 1988a: 149)

The life of the young physically disabled man quoted above could not have been changed without a change in attitudes and practices on the part of those working with him. For those working with older people, changes in attitudes and actions also need to be tackled.

Getting to know the staff

A degree of separation or distance has been typically maintained between staff and residents. This is reflected in staff preoccupations with physical care rather than social interaction. Report after report comments that residents feel 'staff are too busy to talk' or that the home is 'too short-staffed', that staff do not feel that 'just talking' is a legitimate part of their work. This is part of the way in which formal care is seen as work or labour (see Lee-Treweek 1995). There is no evidence that higher rates of staffing lead to greater interaction between staff and residents, and yet residents do value their relationship with staff (Willcocks *et al.* 1987). Distancing is also seen in the way staff may objectify residents rather than see them as real people. The older residents can become bodies to wash, feed and take to the toilet. Again, this routinization of work may be justified by staff as a way of getting through the daily tasks, but we also need to consider the attitudes of staff to their own ageing and the close proximity of death and dying, and how this affects their actions.

Research has shown that residents may be more inclined to engage in conversation and form relationships, albeit tentative, with staff rather than with other residents. Yet, there is evidence that where residents have something in common – a language, a culture, a history – then friendships can develop at this stage in life. Common bonds and shared experiences are important and this becomes one of the reasons why homes which have been set up for particular occupational or religious groups seem to succeed while others fail (Reed and Roskell Payton 1995).

Another area which has featured strongly in much research is the wish for privacy with a room of one's own. While it is recognized that some people wish to share a room and should be so accommodated (see NISW 1988a: 38), they are a minority. The single room has, over the last decade, become a symbol of control which becomes even more meaningful if it contains a person's possessions and if that person is encouraged to use the room as his or her personal base. This means having unimpeded access; and yet large residential homes can take on very public characteristics, with residents spending long periods of time in public places (Willcocks *et al.* 1987) often for the convenience of staff and under watchful – if caring – eyes. Only in small homes, where public space may be minimal, do residents sometimes face the alternative scenario of being marooned for long periods of time alone in their rooms, and not by choice (Weaver *et al.* 1985).

The apparent apathy of many older people, sitting in the public lounges of residential homes, is frequently commented upon. And yet behind the faces sit many lively minds seldom asked to make decisions for themselves because they are deemed incapable. As we have seen above, where residents have shared experiences, they may develop exchanges which go unrecognized by passers-by or busy staff, who remain unaware of this interactivity. For residents, however, being deemed incapable can lead, in time, to a 'learned helplessness' which may become contagious within the collectivity of residents and staff, and compound the process of disempowerment experienced by many during and beyond admission. This could be conceptualized as a cycle of disenchantment.

The environment itself is an important aspect of the residential home as experienced both from within and by outsiders. Within an unfamiliar, and often a large building, residents may find it difficult to orientate themselves to achieve effective use of the new space. This, where it is experienced, is likely to add to their disquiet and exacerbate feelings of lack of control. Yet, there is information to suggest that it is possible to arrange and equip homes in ways which can counter such disorientation and helplessness (Lawton 1980; Hiatt 1980; Greenwell 1989). For instance, those older people suffering from incontinence should be able to find a toilet quickly and so maintain their dignity, and those whose mental frailties have led to behaviour which cannot be managed in a domestic setting must be able to negotiate their new environment without physically endangering themselves.

Considering the home as a part of the wider community raises issues about ways in which residents may remain connected to their past not just in terms of places but also with regard to activities (Elkan and Kelly 1991). Although older people thinking about a move to residential care commonly wish to remain engaged with their former life – their family, friends and outside interests – many residents find themselves living in communities with which they are unfamiliar. The reality of residential life may be different from the expectation.

> The great majority (90 per cent) of people in day centres said that they would want a home to have transport to enable them to go out on trips and visits, and just over three quarters of those questioned (76 per cent) expected a home to provide transport for the use of residents' activities. Alas, only 23 per cent of the residents surveyed lived in homes with transport specifically for their use. Of those who did not have access to transport, almost two-thirds (65 per cent) said that they would have liked this.
>
> (Counsel & Care 1992a: 14)

> Ninety per cent wanted and 83 per cent expected their families to visit; 'I want to be as close as possible to my friends and my son so they can visit', said one respondent hopefully. Alas, the reality for the residents interviewed was that 16 per cent had no family to visit and 7 per cent were never visited by their families. 33 per cent had monthly visits or less, 37 per cent had weekly visits, and 7 per cent had daily visits.
>
> (Counsel & Care 1992a: 20)

Not surprisingly, the residents interviewed in this study were older than the community respondents and, as already noted, would be likely to display different characteristics in terms of health and family support. However, it cannot be acceptable to expect residents to have lower expectations than older people living in the community. It may be that their circumstances generate different priorities, but the research evidence seems to point to the fact that aspects of residential caring may further restrict the lives and aspirations of those who have already experienced significant change; it is the accumulation of these personal degradations which can affect self-esteem.

Residents' rights: the impact of charters, contracts and codes of practice

Messages concerning the negative effects of institutional living are not uncommon. Since the 1970s, one of the ways policy makers and practitioners have responded is to call for an explicit recognition of the rights of residents, supported by the development of philosophies of care which recognize adulthood and citizenship. The work of the Personal Social Services Council (PSSC 1977) encapsulates an early recognition of this approach.

Additionally, by the late 1970s, some local authorities were beginning to draw up charters of rights. Norman (1980: 46) gives the example of the charter drawn up by East Sussex County Council in 1979 which highlights a number of points now commonplace in codes of practice. These include a concern with:

• quality of life
• personal independence
• informed choice
• responsible risk-taking
• dignity
• personal privacy
• respect for individuality and personal history
• consultation and decision-making
• maintenance of control over life-style
• access to facilities
• right to the acceptance of cultural, sexual, religious and emotional needs
• community involvement
• rights as citizens

The move towards codifying the underlying principles upon which residential practice should be based has been driven by a number of diverse influences, both positive and negative. One key element has been catastrophe and scandal, the bad press given to residential care. A positive driver has been the more recent development of National Vocational Qualifications for care workers. The privatization of residential care, the most recent diversification of providers and, to a lesser extent, of services, and the increased role of regulation in monitoring standards and quality cannot be ignored. Below is a good example of a 'rights check-list' to be found in the Kent County Council (1991: 7) document, *Good Care*:

Service users have a right to a quality of service. This means:

• choosing how they want to be addressed;
• having access to a range of specialist services;
• choosing what they want to eat;
• having access to an advocate;
• being treated as an individual.

Service users have a right to belong in their home. This means:

- privacy in their own room;
- consultation about any changes in living arrangements;
- being able to suggest improvements;
- having visitors of their choice;
- having a residency agreement that is clearly laid out;
- knowing their belongings are safe;
- having their own room unless otherwise requested.

Service users have a right to citizenship. This means:

- registering and voting in elections;
- mixing with local community;
- choosing their own GP and dentist;
- being independent without unnecessary restrictions;
- having respect for their cultural and religious needs;
- caring for themselves wherever possible.

The sentiments contained in this listing are echoed in other prestigious documents such as *Home Life* (CPA 1984) and *A Better Home Life* (CPA 1996), *Residential Care: A Positive Choice* (NISW 1988a) and *Residential Care: Positive Answers* (NISW 1993), and *Homes are for Living In* (DoH 1989b). What they all have in common is the emphasis on valuing the lives of individuals and enabling them to maintain continuity of purpose and opportunities to contribute during a period of change. There is an increasing and explicit acknowledgement of the shared nature of residential care. We would argue that if the tension between the individual and collective aspects of residential care is well managed, then shared living need not become the 'institutionalization' which often prevents residents from achieving personal autonomy in residential care.

To achieve shared living where residents, staff and relatives are equals, though with differing resources to contribute – in terms of skills, knowledge and experience – is not easy. It demands a recognition not only of the unequal power relations which exist between the parties involved, but also that each group may feel powerless to create change. The result is a stereotype of marginalized older residents, poorly valued, untrained care staff; and exhausted informal carers. It is the reason why the Wagner report states: 'It is true that what we have to say has been said many times before; the question remains, why has it not been consistently translated into practice' (NISW 1988a: 61).

This begs the question: are 'charters of residents' rights' and 'codes of practice' simply rhetoric to which lip-service is paid? Such charters aim to ensure that older people maintain the rights they had when they lived in the community, but how far have those older people who become residents already lost some of these rights? Codes of practice embody ideals that residents are not treated as 'less than whole people', but such ideals are not enforceable in a direct legislative sense. Certainly there have been changes in practices in some homes, with key worker systems and care planning programmes aimed at supporting older people as individuals, where residents are enabled to maintain their personal level of participation, and where there is some recognition of the need for people to integrate their past and present lives. The value base underlying the system for care workers is partly founded on these principles.

Codes of practice have also formed a foundation for tools of quality control and quality assurance. The conditions for the registering of a residential or nursing home rest with the Registered Homes Act 1984, and the need for 'fit' persons to run a home, 'fit' buildings to house a home, 'fit' care plans as a guide to how the home is to be run. But inspection provides only one perspective on life in homes (Kellaher *et al.* 1988; Day *et al.* 1996). As a part of the Caring for People package, the NHS and Community Care Act 1990 introduced a require-ment that all homes should have a carefully developed complaints system which residents should be actively encouraged to use (DoH 1989a).

In recent years those who own and manage homes have expressed inter-est in the potential value of self-regulation and various plans have been devel-oped which enable staff to assess their own performance and for managers to understand the training requirements of their staff. Documents such as *Homes are For Living In* (DoH 1989b) or *Evaluating the Quality of Care* (Payne 1994) are underpinned by philosophies of care which centre on staff attitudes. Others, such as Total Quality Management (DTI 1991) or work around the British Standard BS 5750 are more concerned with the organizational structures and systems which support the care work in a home. To date, particularly in relation to work with older people, the *Inside Quality Assurance* system (CESSA 1992) alone insists that residents should be placed centrally in decision-making about change within a home (see Kellaher and Peace 1993).

Both the NISW training programme (Payne 1994) and the *Inside Quality Assurance* programme were developed as part of the Department of Health's Caring in Homes Initiative of 1989–93, which funded four programmes based on demonstration projects around the issues of staff training, quality assur-ance, community liaison/integration and information needs (Youll and McCourt-Perring 1993). The aim of this programme was to develop an appro-priate set of enabling frameworks that represented a response to the Wagner report's recommendations. The intention was to guide the new purchasers and providers of residential care who must respond in relation to local cir-cumstances.

Of course, the success or failure of programmes which seek to bring about change within residential settings cannot be divorced from changes in the community and society as a whole. We have already commented on the paucity of community alternatives for support for older people and how this can influence the pathways and manner of entry into residential care. The nature of tenure or residency, along with permanence in residential life, further suggest a limited influence or control on the basic aspect of residence. It is interesting that while the Wagner report recommended that residents should have a 'written contract of accommodation and services between the resident (or their agent) and the provider' (NISW 1988a: 37) and guidance has been given in *Positive Answers* (NISW 1993) such contracts are still not universal.

Kent County Council (1991: 21) suggests the following as part of good management:

When someone moves into your home they lose the security that most people take for granted. If it is expected that the move is to be permanent it is good practice to give as much security as possible through a residency agreement. This will specify the rights of occupation which you are giving along with the conditions which are expected to be observed. It would also set out how you and the service user would agree to change those conditions if necessary.

The immense upheaval in the provision and funding of long-term care services throughout the 1980s and into the 1990s has meant that for some older people permanency is uncertain. It can depend not only on their own personal and family financial circumstances but also on market fluctuations and local and health authority commitments.

It is clear from this discussion, and from the review of the research, that attempts to make explicit the rights of older residents and what they can expect from residential practice are an expression of the possibility of change. Such developments, however, can be a cover for providers and policy-makers where the realities of practice and the role of residential care are not also made explicit and part of the negotiation.

Interdependency in residential care: maintaining autonomy, acknowledging dependency

So far we have seen that certain older people may be more likely to move into residential homes than others and that the transition itself can present a serious challenge to such older people's need to preserve identity through maintaining vital connections in their former lives. Such transitions – fragile in themselves – can become precarious because of the workings of the residential system which, as a business organization, has other demands to meet apart from the care needs of individual older people. The care ideal must be translated into paid work which is ambiguously valued by society; the environment can become a place of efficiency and cleanliness; the idiosyncratic routines of everyday life can be subverted by the need for order and structure. It is unsurprising then, that the basic theme of much research in the UK and elsewhere (see Hofland 1988) is that the processes of becoming a resident and of living in institutional settings can undermine personal influence, leading to negative effects on 'emotional, physical and behavioural well-being'. That institutions become divorced from the wider communities in which they are located, and that older residents become insignificant, may not be surprising but it cannot pass unchallenged.

The nature of connectedness between people's past and present lives may well be crucial in the social adjustment to residential living. Hence, a better understanding of the complex relationship between autonomy and dependency experienced by each individual throughout the life course must be sought. Gender, race, class and disability, and age itself, will inevitably influence such interrelationships.

While ageism may affect all age groups, a youth-oriented culture with a power base in youth and middle age means that the impact of ageism is most likely to be felt among the very young and those over pensionable age (Johnson and Bytheway 1993). The ageism which devalues and marginalizes older people can be seen as a gradual but invasive process which is frequently internalized. Older people become devalued in terms of access to resources; ignored as people with a contribution to make; and made invisible as bodies in decline (Agich 1993; Bytheway 1995). This represents a set of circumstances which is arguably more acute for older women – the majority of those who move into care settings. That covert and explicit forms of ageism are experienced at a time of material and multiple loss is a reality which needs to be appreciated by those who work with older people at the end of their lives. There also needs to be a recognition that organizations, and the way in which they interact with older people, can contribute to rather than reduce dependency. This may apply within domestic situations as well as in a residential home (Gavilan 1990) but the collective and organized character of life in institutions can amplify a fragile situation, making it visible (see Norman 1980) and, indeed, may come to symbolize the delicate balance of dependence and autonomy.

It is against this background that the increasing emphasis being placed on the rights of residents needs to be considered, for if the ideals about resident rights are to be translated into practice they must address more complex notions than has hitherto been the case, of interactions between dependency and autonomy and what is really meant by interdependency. Dixon (1991) approached the issue of institutional dependency through a piece of action research in one residential home. She found that the dispositions of a proportion of the staff, who saw residents as 'less than whole persons', proved a difficult attitudinal barrier to cross, and she concluded that the paternalism which exists in residential settings is rooted within ageist attitudes which persist in society generally. Thus, professionals seek to protect residents rather than invite, as they see it, problems through permitting the taking of reasonable risks, and in doing so take away the responsibility of the individual for his or her own life.

> Residential care itself can be seen as an expression of 'Less Than Whole Person' (the resident being seen as no longer able to cope) and although 'Really Normal' noises may be made ('it is the residents' own home and we must treat it as such') the philosophy of the home in reality will probably be 'Enlightened Guardianship', with the emphasis being on realistic adjustment as defined by staff. 'Disabled Power' seems by definition to be incompatible with current residential provision and certainly one meets few residents who assert that old is beautiful and that it is society and the staff who are handicapping them. Perhaps they would not last very long in the home if they did.
>
> (Dixon 1991: 88)

If this is the reality, then what can be done to reinstate independence in old age in the residential setting? The work of the American writer, B.J. Collopy, is illuminating and helpful as he unpicks the complexity of autonomy:

> autonomy is defined as a notional field, a loose system of interorbiting

Figure 3.3   Collopy's polarities within autonomy

1 **Decisional v. executional**
   Having preferences, making decision v. being able to implement
   them or carry them out.
2 **Direct v. delegated**
   Deciding or acting on one's own v. giving authority to others to
   decide/act on your behalf.
3 **Competent v. incapacitated**
   Reasonable and judgementally coherent choice/activity v. that
   which exhibits rational defect or judgemental incoherence.
4 **Authentic v. inauthentic**
   Choices/actions which are constant with character v. those which
   are seriously out of character.
5 **Immediate v. long range**
   Present or limited expressions of autonomy v. future or wide-
   ranging expressions.
6 **Negative v. positive**
   Choice/activity that claims a right only to non-interference v. that
   which claims positive entitlement, support, capacitation.

Source: adapted from Collopy (1988: 11).

concepts that tract out the varied paths of self-determination. Accordingly, autonomy is understood as a cluster of notions including self-
determination, freedom, independence, liberty of choice and action. In
its most general terms, autonomy signifies control or decision-making
and other activity by the individual. It refers to human agency free of
outside intervention and interference.

(Collopy 1988: 10)

He also disentangles various polarities and dimensions (Figure 3.3) which
make up the concept of autonomy and considers these as they apply in everyday life in long-term care settings. Breaking down the complexities of autonomy in this way provides some starting points. Negative and positive
autonomy set the issue in the most stark contrast. By negative autonomy is
meant the right to claim freedom from any interference. This is obviously an
untenable position for most older people living in residential care – unless
their admission has been occasioned through a need solely for accommodation without care. The 'care' aspect demands some form of 'interference'
but positive autonomy would construe this as enabling rather than as controlling, and given as a right which confers status on the individual. Enabling
rather than controlling autonomy may permit individuals to develop, rather
than being restricted to limited expressions of who they are and what they
wish to accomplish. This is what is entailed in the continuum which extends
from immediate to long-term autonomy.

Beginning from this basis, it seems to be important to consider whether expressions of autonomy are authentic or inauthentic – whether the actions or choices made by the older person are in character or at odds with character. The recognition of authenticity implies an understanding and acknowledgement of the individual's life history, either directly or through an advocacy/third-party relationship. It seems that only through a lens which permits some assessment of what is authentic – or not – for a particular individual can judgements be made about competency and the delegation or execution of decisions. Such judgements should lead to a valid form of interdependency which can be reflected in decisional and executional forms of action and of direct as compared to delegated autonomy. In this connection it needs to be noted that in *Residential Care: Positive Answers* (NISW 1993: 70–4) the point is made that the approach to care which recognizes the value of individuals regardless of age appears to be a feature which is common in accounts of residential care which have been initiated by black groups for older black people.

Taking on board the depth of relationship between residents and carers required to explore the complexity of autonomy/dependency as outlined in Collopy's work, demands a practice base which places value on one-to-one working, continuity, time, listening, and a regard for shared care (family or other third-party involvement). It must also acknowledge that many residents will die in residential homes and that the fear of care workers about their own ageing and death can present further barriers to such shared understanding. In Part Two of this book we explore further whether the residential home of today has the capability and capacity to meet this challenge or whether it is merely a structure for introducing, containing, managing or possibly exacerbating dependencies.

Notes

1 This study was based on interviews with 100 older people who were asked what they would want from the ideal residential care home if they were to ever be in need of one, and a further 100 older people who were asked what they expected a home would be like if they went into one. These respondents were all people attending voluntary and local authority day centres in London. Also interviewed were 100 residents in 54 homes in 20 inner and outer London boroughs (see Counsel & Care 1992a: 8–11).

PART II

Debating the issues

4

Care and control

In the second part of this book the intention is to build on the factual information, historical evidence and research findings which we have considered
in Part I. We reflect on what this says about residential care and its place, in
the mid-1990s, in the range of social interventions available to older people
towards the end of their lives. We approach this in the form of three separate
but related essays which build up towards a reconceptualization of residential
care at the end of the twentieth century. We are concerned with changes in
the role of residential care in society, the form and function of homes on the
ground and the ways in which care arrangements reflect societal unease
about demographic change and an inability to confront, with confidence, the
presence of death and dying; hence, the institutional options which aim to
control the phenomena of ageing but may (inadvertently or advisedly) culminate in the control of older people themselves.

We begin with a consideration of the arguments identified in Chapter 1
(Baldwin *et al.* 1993). These concern the way in which the residential care
home, while being a system which has a clear and valid function – to care
and support those who cannot manage in the ordinary domestic setting – may
also be construed as a form of social control which restricts the lives of older
people who become residents and, arguably as potential residents, all older
people. Baldwin *et al.* argue that older people entering residential care are
already victims of actions and dispositions which devalue age in many
Western – if not other – societies and that the residential setting does not, of
itself, exert this detrimental influence. If we accept that older people living in
residential homes are, or have been, at least as vulnerable to these pressures
as their counterparts in the community, then we might proceed to argue as
follows: either the structures which support and surround residential organizations are immaterial and make things neither better nor worse; or the
complex factors which determine the shape and style of residential living are

distinct from those which influence life for older people in the community and exert an additional set of influences which devalue older people still further as they become residents.

As we have seen in Part I, certain groups of older people – women, those most mentally frail, those living alone, and those who have been hospitalized – may become predisposed to a move into residential or nursing home care. The dislocation from familiar people, habits and surroundings may in itself be an undermining experience, often removing the options for older people to maintain connections and continuities in their lives and to make their contribution to family, community and society. Such serious dislocations can be exacerbated by the organizational, social and physical environments which were characteristic of most residential homes in our earlier study of local authority provision. The extent to which environments are now more varied and less characterized by such dislocating features has yet to be shown.

For some older people a move to residential care may be viewed positively. The vulnerability which may be experienced in community settings may be such as to make the move both acceptable and manageable. It may be argued that enhanced care in the community should remove the need for such moves, but for some older people not only a precarious set of domestic circumstances but also a sense of alienation from their community and from society may make the refuge of a supported residential environment attractive. There is also some evidence (see Chapter 3) that where people find a common bond with the group they join, collective living can be a positive experience. In order to pursue these debates and lines of argument more fully we need now to explore a number of related issues and deal with several questions which are fundamental to an understanding of the future forms which residential care may assume.

Firstly, is the residential care home a societal institution which provides a place for people who are regarded as deviant? If that is the case, are we to regard the residential enterprise as an agent of the state which regulates the pressure exerted on families to provide care at home, rather than to label their elders, and by association themselves, as deviant?

Secondly, is the residential care home of today still seen in the same light as the workhouse? If this is not the case, is it because society has changed, and with it the needs, expectations and aspirations of potential residents, or because residential care has changed to meet newly recognized needs? These questions lead us to ask, finally, whether the residential care home is now an anachronism or whether its role has evolved over time.

The extent to which we can argue the case for one or other of these propositions has implications for future residential directions. Is there a need to develop more responsive alternatives which permit the reduction of residential care by providing more care at home, diverse housing options and increased nursing input? (This question will be pursued in Chapter 5.) Is there room for any such manoeuvres, or are we just obliged to preserve and promote our costly residential inheritance, entailing, as it does, investment in buildings, in people and their support and training – to say nothing of an ideology? In the present economic system it may be too difficult to dismantle the residential edifice without radical change. In order to explore these challenging questions we begin by considering the residential care home as a form of social control.

Institutions as regulators: power without

There is a well-developed literature concerning the role of institutions – such as prisons, mental hospitals and residential establishments for all groups of people – as places where those deemed dangerous or marginal to society are best secluded (Ignatieff 1983; Jones and Fowles 1984). Such institutions, whatever their scale, convey strong messages not only about how society organizes itself but also about how it groups and values people. In this literature, residential care homes and hospital settings for older people have featured significantly (Barton 1959; Robb 1967) with the work of Peter Townsend (1962; 1972; 1981; 1986) being the most influential. However, much of the debate concerning institutions as regulators uses the prison or mental hospital as its example.

While we might review a range of texts to convey something of the strength of this wider debate, we look first at two theoreticians, Michel Foucault and Erving Goffman, who have been particularly influential in examining the role of institutions and their function in society, at micro and macro levels. Foucault's thinking and the debate he generated are located at the macro-societal level. He was primarily concerned with structure and, while he wrote about mental hospitals (*Madness and Civilisation*, 1967) and prisons (*Discipline and Punish*, 1973), his concern was not for these establishments in themselves but for the way they convey messages about control and influence over individuals and groups. Foucault's analysis is that the message is one of power and that institutions are used in certain ways – direct and indirect, explicit and implicit – by the powerful to control groups which lack power. He rejected the humanistic view that the autonomous and rational individual is the source of social meaning; rather he saw people's lives as socially determined and 'produced through social discourses (language, thought, symbolic representation) which position subjects in a field of power relations and within particular sets of practices' (quoted in Layder 1994: 95).

Foucault believed that humanism overstressed the degree of control which people can exert over their lives. In his terms, the residential setting would be construed as a manifestation of certain power relations and the practices of residential caring, in the broadest sense, would then be seen as forms of control; control, that is, over those judged to be without reason. It is interesting that within *Discipline and Punish* Foucault illustrated that punishment, as a public spectacle, or as an event which the community watched and judged, had, by the end of the eighteenth century, been replaced by the 'hidden process' of punishment through imprisonment, which was inflicted through judgements which were made on an individualized basis (Jones and Fowles 1984). Such a view can be paralleled in the residential home which, in its most closed state, enables abuse against older people to go unheeded (Biggs *et al.* 1995).

Although Foucault and Goffman were writing about institutions at around the same time – in the 1960s – albeit on different sides of the Atlantic, there was little cross-fertilization between their ideas and writing. Goffman, a sociologist, also studied the mental hospital and the prison within *Asylums* (1961), and they became the vehicle for his main intellectual interest: symbolic interactionism. In focusing on the perceptions of 'inmates' rather than of staff, organization or management, he considered those features of institutions which deprive, constrain and control individual lives, outlining in four essays those aspects of the 'total' or 'most closed' type of institution which constitute a Weberian 'ideal type' (see Figure 3.3).

> First, all aspects of life are conducted in the same place and under the same single authority. Second, each phase of the members daily activity is carried on in the immediate company of a large batch of others, all of whom are treated alike and required to do the same things together. Third, all phases of the day's activities are tightly scheduled, with one activity leading at a pre-arranged time into the next, the whole sequence of activities being imposed from above by a system of explicit formal rulings and a body of officials. Finally, the various enforced activities are brought together into a single rational plan purportedly designed to fulfil the official aims of the institution.
>
> (Goffman 1961: 17)

He did not suggest that all institutions had these features but drew together enough observations to make a convincing case, which remains influential. Indeed, he was one of the first to champion the user perspective.

However, Jones and Fowles (1984: 25–6) note, Goffman did not intend this abstraction to be understood and applied as the sum total of the reality, and his work was a guide for action:

> Within our frame of reference, it must be recognised as partial evidence: it outlines an ideal type (which is an extreme case), it concentrates on inmate views and ignores policy issues, it is based on highly selective data, it stresses similarities and ignores differences and it shows little understanding of the problems of severely abnormal behaviour, or of running a stigmatised and underfinanced service.

Goffman, like Foucault, was concerned not so much with the individual as with the way in which deviant groups were formed and how such deviancy was used in the construction of symbols which had the effect of setting and then maintaining the norms of groups, communities and society itself – a theme he pursued further in *Stigma* (1963). Hence the view that 'institutions such as prisons or mental hospitals are necessary in order for us all to strive to keep out of them'. Goffman's work is important in enabling us to make the links between micro and macro levels of analysis, moving from observations of everyday life to the implications for society. He helps us to consider the double effects of the power and control which institutions in their widest sense can have in regulating actions both within them and beyond, in community and society.

The views of these two writers, even though their work has not been specifically concerned with older people living in residential settings, offer influential perspectives on the complexity and extent of power and control which rests in institutions, of which residential and nursing homes are but one form.

The question then arises as to how applicable these ideas may be to the residential home as we now perceive it. Certainly, the issue of control could be seen in the widespread fear of the workhouse commonly reported by older people earlier in this century and may still be reflected in the accepted norm, based on their own statements, that older people wish 'to remain at home for as long as possible'. Times have changed, however, and the workhouse and the associated coercion may no longer be the lens through which contemporary cohorts of older people regard residential settings. A more common expression regarding the reason for admission to care homes is 'not to be a burden on family members'. This sense of burden is crucial to our discussion. That older people should feel burdensome at the end of their lives is indicative of their position both as individuals and as members of a group, in a society which places differentiated social and economic value on its citizens. The residential care home, therefore, may have become a symbol of institutionalized ageism. Alternatively, the desire not to be a burden may merely reflect the long tradition of independent living within British society.

Residential care as a form of institutionalized ageism

Townsend's seminal work, *The Last Refuge*, was discussed in Chapter 1. There we cited Townsend, in 1962, questioning the role of residential care homes (see p. 10), and making recommendations which should bring about their demise. His arguments were supported by a set of principles comprising: self-determination, respect for the individual, maintenance of health, preservation of residential independence, the right to an occupation, social security, social opportunity, security of income, and social equality. These elements have much in common with the 'Declaration of Intent' of the Pensioners' Convention first outlined in 1979. It was the absence of such a possibility, for a charter of entitlement, which inspired Townsend's theory of structured dependence, first presented in a paper for the launch edition of *Ageing and Society* in 1981 (Townsend 1981).

While Townsend (1962: 328–70) offers ample evidence of the effects of institutionalization upon individuals, he was not concerned to the same extent with issues of practice. His analysis centred around residential care as a discrete aspect of social policy. He wanted to bring about change in the provision of care for older people and produced specific and actionable recommendations. His subsequent concerns lie with the position of older people in society and the role of residential care, alongside the imposition and, generally forced, acceptance of earlier retirement. This in turn is seen to legitimate low income and thereby to culminate in socially manufactured dependency. Thus, older people become dependent, in all aspects of social interaction, because their options and life chances are institutionally restricted. Townsend challenged researchers for failing to question the fundamental 'why?' of residential care and for accepting 'the existence of contemporary and social institutions as inevitable and necessary' (Townsend 1981: 8). The research questions which had been tackled, he suggests, had been along the lines of 'How can the burden for relatives and the state be lightened, or how can the administration of institutional care be made more efficient?' (Townsend 1981: 6). Explanations as to the causes and rationales for the shape and style of residential provision had not, suggested Townsend, been sought through research. In so far as fundamental explanations had been sought or produced, these had been at the level of the individual and their adjustments to the change which residential life represented, rather than at the level of society, its structures, influences and effects. Peter Townsend concluded his 1981 article with a forceful attack on the failure to develop creative community care, and says this about residential care:

> The failure to shift the balance of health and welfare policy towards community care also has to be explained in relation to the function of institutions to regulate and confirm inequality in society, and indeed to regulate deviation from the central social values of self-help, domestic independence, personal thrift, willingness to work, productive effort and family care. Institutions serve subtle functions in reflecting the positive structural and cultural changes taking place in society.
>
> (Townsend 1981: 22)

Thus Townsend, in common with Foucault and Goffman, cites the power of the residential institution to regulate, but where he differs from them is in his concern with inequality. Townsend's views are pertinent, closer to home, and they merit close consideration. In 1986, he elaborated his theme, arguing that:

> The dependency of the elderly has been 'structured' by long-term economic and social policies: elderly people are perceived and treated as more dependent than they are or need to be by the state, and this outcome has been fostered by the rapidly developing institutions of retirement, income maintenance, residential and domiciliary care, which comprise a subordinate but necessary part of the overall management of state policy.
>
> (Townsend 1986: 15)

Here Townsend starts to articulate a form of social deviancy which is attributed to older people. Rather than seeing residential care as a form of intervention which sets out to alleviate individual problems and meet individual needs, he considers residential care as a form of social policy which demonstrates institutionalized ageism, that is, a service which articulates discrimination against people on the basis of their chronological age. It is part of a process, legitimated through policy, which, alongside mandatory retirement and pensions policies, serves to marginalize older people, stripping them of the right – and opportunity – to participate fully in society.

The processes around residential organization represent one pathway by which dependency is socially created and reproduced. The currency of care is dependency, a fact further endorsed by professionals and the wider public through prevailing attitudes and beliefs about old age. However, underlying all forms of ageism is what Bytheway describes as 'a biological basis for social discrimination between living people' (Bytheway 1982: 391). Later,

Bytheway and Johnson (1990: 36–7) offer the following, broader definition of ageism:

1 Ageism is a set of beliefs originating in the biological variation between people and relating to the ageing process.
2 It is in the actions of corporate bodies, what is said and done by their representatives, and the resulting views that are held by ordinary ageing people, that ageism is manifest.

In consequence of this, it follows that:

(a) Ageism generates and reinforces a fear and denigration of the ageing process, and stereotyping presumptions regarding competence and the need for protection.
(b) In particular, ageism legitimates the use of chronological age to mark out classes of people who are systematically denied resources and opportunities that others enjoy, and who suffer the consequences of such denigration, ranging from well-meaning patronage to unambiguous vilification.

Townsend sees the consequences of ageism revealed in the acquiescence of welfare professionals and their tendency readily to offer institutional care:

> Confronted with disabled people who are also elderly, social workers do not assume they have the means to overcome their problems themselves and do not resort to the advocacy of self-reliant strategies. And there is a tendency to see admission to an institution as a more desirable step than the evidence would warrant.
>
> (Townsend 1986: 31)

Such actions reflect Bytheway & Johnson's assertion that ageism is 'rooted in the biological variation between people', with health and welfare workers failing to see the unique older person behind the ageing process.

For Townsend, writing in 1986, residential homes, which accommodate only a minority of older people, have a wider significance. They 'symbolise the dependence of the elderly and legitimate their lack of access to equality of status' (Townsend 1986: 32). This argument is supported by evidence which Townsend cites about the 'capacities of residents' and 'social restriction or authoritarian styles of management'. He reviewed research carried out in local authority homes between 1958 and 1982, and with regard to the 'capacities of residents' he concludes that :

(i) a substantial minority (perhaps two-fifths) of elderly residents can undertake most or all self-care tasks; assessments of their capacities contradicting the idea that they are 'in need of care and attention';
(ii) the proportion of elderly residents who are capable of undertaking most or all self-care tasks has diminished in the last 20 years but not as substantially as often supposed by administrators and staff, and does not appear to have shown signs of further diminishing in the

last five years, despite the high average age of residents in many homes;

(iii) contrariwise, a minority of residents are very severely disabled. There is little sign of administrative success in placing such severely disabled people, many of whom require medical and nursing or hospital care, quickly enough in the geriatric residential or day-care facilities which they need, or that appropriate specialist services are made available where they live.

(Townsend 1986: 33)

Thus the case is made that some people do not need residential care while others need more support than can be offered. This evidence is in line with our 1981 data which showed that around a third of residents (35 per cent of women and 29 per cent of men) explained their presence in a residential home because of not being able to manage any longer at home due to ill health or having had an accident. However, more recently, as we saw in Chapter 3, research has stressed the importance of living alone; the need for intensive support at home; and the presence of dementia in determining risk of admission to care (Opit and Pahl 1993). There is evidence, then, of a change in circumstances surrounding coming into a care home, although there is still a diversity of residents.

The picture painted by Townsend is one where staff collude with this mix of residents, needing to keep a 'manageable level of care' because 'levels of staffing and the organisation of daily routine do not allow the number of very severely disabled residents to exceed a kind of "tolerance" level' (Townsend 1986: 36). Today, such collusion may not be possible. This raises important issues for staff and indicates the pressures that need to be managed by the formal carer, to which we return shortly. Such issues are not addressed by Townsend who sees the solution in terms of a 'single form of residence for the most severely disabled and measures taken to ensure that the less disabled live in homes of their own with supporting services' (Townsend 1986: 42).

Institutions as controllers: power within

For Townsend, the residential home is not just a powerful, highly visible and explicit symbol for those who remain outside its boundaries; he regards the internal organization as controlling those within the setting itself. This, in turn, he views as inducing further dependency and beyond even the most radical change. In noting attempts throughout the 1970s and into the 1980s to create more personalized regimes within homes, he considers a range of research findings (including our own) but detects 'an ideology of "care and attention" rather than the encouragement of self-help and self-management'. He concludes with a quote from Booth's (1985: 207) study of local authority homes in the north east 'the findings of this study suggest that the detrimental effects of residential living cannot be allayed within the bounds of current residential practice'. The investment in levels of staffing, which are costly if still inadequate, in staff training, and in resources and facilities, he argues, reflects the low status of the residents.

As we saw in Chapter 3, many researchers have adopted Goffman's 'characteristics of total institutions' to highlight the many ways in which an institutional regime may control the lives of those who live and work there. As we have already shown (Peace *et al.* 1982; Willcocks *et al.* 1987) the residential home, as a community for living and a place to work, combines the complex tasks of providing for 'private lives in public places'. This complexity is seen most clearly in the continuous tension around personal autonomy, control and risk taking for residents, and staff anxiety about, and responsibility for, safety and accountability. While Booth's work, cited above, and our own analysis of local authority homes in the early 1980s revealed little significant variation between homes and the ways these tensions were managed (Willcocks *et al.* 1987), the overall style of life within homes can vary from those which can be said to be 'more open' to those which are 'more closed'.

It is this capacity of residential organizations to become self-contained which Biggs *et al.* (1995: 78) suggest leads to 'secretiveness, suspicion of the outside and a lack of accountability'. They add: 'when the pressures of work, both personal and institutional, dominate residents' requirements, in a closed environment with scant respect for resident autonomy and privacy, mistreatment is always waiting in the wings'. Whilst the authors question the view of institutional care as, in itself, abusive, they acknowledge certain features of institutional culture which may lead to systems which are likely to be more abusive and controlling. These might include: lack of management goals; negative staff attitudes; lack of staff training; low staff morale; lack of resources; and the low status of care work (see Phillipson and Biggs 1992). In situations where 'the usual moral inhibitions against violence become weakened' (Kelman 1973: 38, cited in Biggs *et al.* 1995: 83) then they suggest care may be corrupted. Such situations can occur where residents are stripped of personal identity; where staff resolve their own low status by asserting their power over residents. Moreover, where management systems and organizational routines lack transparency and purpose, with participation and self-criticism being stifled, abuse may occur (Wardhaugh and Wilding 1993). Elder abuse in care settings has not received as much attention as abuse in domestic settings, an omission which Biggs *et al.* (1995) see as a consequence of the development of a mixed economy of residential and nursing home care and the emergence of sophisticated regulatory systems for care settings. However, they also argue for systems which encourage openness and resident participation, so that people are confident that complaints procedures and regulation will work in their best interests. They conclude:

> Openness to user participation within establishments, an active and independent advocacy network, and frequent contact with the world outside an institution would be positive signs that a non-abusive culture has developed. Workplace climate and morale have also been identified as key elements in determining whether mistreatment will take place.
>
> (Biggs *et al.* 1995: 91)

If openness is seen as a positive challenge to the control culture, then we should consider the circumstances which render older people reluctant to involve themselves in commenting on life in care, or to adopt a critical stance about their experiences; this is often referred to as a failure to 'speak out' or 'let on'. Speaking out or perhaps whistle-blowing might be seen as a rational approach to expressing views, but typically the nearest that a resident might come to this is to drop hints in terms of 'the staff are very busy', or, more cryptically, 'some funny things go on here' (see Booth 1993; Kellaher and Peace 1993).

One major deterrent to residents speaking out may be the professional ethos of the home and its professional carers. If the residents were to participate in decision-making about the way things happen, might this not represent a challenge to staff, with their accumulated experiences, their training and their specialist knowledge? In other words, they are the people who 'know best' – and they may not take kindly to alternative views being put forward. Additionally, reticence may be exacerbated by communication difficulties between residents and care staff – difficulties based on both cultural and inter-generational differences and/or the practical issues of sensory or physical impairments. Importantly, effective social interaction between different groups with their different interests and concerns may be influenced substantially by the level of debate in a given home about equal opportunities and the presence or absence of an anti-discriminatory framework – most importantly, whether equal opportunities are a tangible force in terms of everyday activities and experiences in the home.

Finally, we must recognize the existence of a range of vested interests and that among these there are some powerful social actors who may need to believe that care arrangements are satisfactory: such interested parties might include heads of services, boards of trustees, care home owners, or chairs of social services committees. For the very best of reasons, in what they believe to be the very best of ways, they have established the various professional care services on behalf of a wider public. We recognize that such groups carry a huge burden and that they invest substantially in the management of their agencies. Hence, any challenge to these arrangements – serious or trivial – can represent an unacceptable undermining of the whole edifice of care. And this in turn may explain the difficulties that we have witnessed when care systems are challenged, either from within or by outsiders.

This begs the question whether there can ever be an acceptable channel for criticism under such circumstances. So, before we address ways of constructing this 'acceptable face of critical comment', it may be helpful to look briefly at the possible consequences of letting on – and why old people themselves prefer to keep their peace.

At the present time, the most likely effect of unacceptable criticism hitting the system is that the system itself will go into a state of shock. At an institutional level there may be denial, defensiveness and an unwillingness to accept the validity of the consumer critique; at a carer level, there is frequently disbelief and a sense of hurt that a resident could pass critical comment.

From the resident's perspective there are a range of consequences, varying in magnitude, when criticisms get into the system.

• There is the chance that the resident might be bullied or victimized: the

slow answering of a bell, the delay in being served tea; the bath too hot or cold; the failure to get an empty commode.
- There is also the possibility of exposure to public view and comment, whereby the resident's own characteristics or behaviour may come under scrutiny; here the complainant must feel secure in her blamelessness.
- Linked to this is the possibility of escalation and a scandal of frightening proportions.
- The resident may fear that ingratitude could lead to her being moved elsewhere; she could be asked or required to leave. This fear may exist irrespective of the possibility of it actually happening.
- The resident may fear a repetition of previous racial or sexual harassment.
- The resident may fear that no one will talk to her or trust her any longer if she 'lets on' – thereby bringing about her own social isolation.
- Or, the resident may simply assume that nothing will happen, that no one will take any notice of what she says.

It is for these reasons that a culture of not letting on or not being critical tends to develop. And this can be extremely difficult to penetrate. Yet it is possible that letting on may engender beneficial outcomes and that a critical comment may lead to positive change and an enhancement of care services and of the resulting quality of life. The challenge to the policy-maker is to provide a structure for letting on that maximizes these benefits.

Residents: deviants and devalued

If social policy is one of the important ways through which society is both constructed and managed, then residential care for older people, as a form of social policy, shapes attitudes towards and beliefs about older people and old age. If the lines of argument which have been outlined are accepted, residents can be seen as representing some of the most marginalized and 'deviant'. Despite what we know of the heterogeneity of resident populations, their castigation as marginal or deviant groups may be extended to all older people. They are deemed to have failed 'assessment tests' of 'self-help, domestic independence, personal thrift, willingness to work, productive effort and family care' (Townsend 1986: 42). In terms of family care and resources, as we have noted in Chapter 2, residents are more likely to include the never married, widowed and childless, but they are also likely to be very old women with limited financial resources and to include those who have experienced many forms of loss – of health, of home, of spouse, of sibling, of partners and of companions.

While we might agree with Townsend that residential care can be construed as a form of institutionalized ageism, contributing to the structured dependency of older people, we are also aware of Bytheway and Johnson's contention that ageism is overdetermined by the visibility of biological decline and that the experience of ageing generates a fear of that process in those who age, but perhaps more so in those who are not yet old. For older people, loss of health, and the possibility of having to deal with marked physical and mental decline, are arguably the most threatening experience to the self and to identity (see Hepworth 1995). The association of institutional life with increased dependency, occasioned and revealed through ill health, is likely to act as a powerful threat within and beyond the ageing population, so that those who are able to manage their lives at home dissociate themselves from those who have 'given in' to institutional living. Researchers often find that older people do not respond very fully to questions about their plans for the future, freely admitting that 'they do not want to think about it'. Indeed, even within residential institutions, the more able residents are likely to dissociate themselves from less able residents.

In a recent article Hepworth (1995) cites the work of authors writing about social problems and deviancy to show how old age can be viewed as a problem through displaced fear of the ageing process and, ultimately, of death (see, for example, Woodward 1991). This displacement, he argues, generates categories which run between the 'normal' (those defined as un-old, or undying) to the 'deviant' (those deemed closest to death through age). In turn, the need for institutional solutions, which support – and redefine – such categories, arises. He comments:

> At the present time the strategy favoured by both professionals and lay persons is to transform later life into an extended middle age terminating in a quick and painless exit: 'dying on time' as it is sometimes called. The associated practice is firstly to transform the physical problems associated with the biological changes of later life (disability, confusion, social incompetence) firstly into social deviance – a process inevitably implying if not explicitly requiring moral discrimination and judgement. Secondly, to transform deviance in later life into evidence of social and (preferably) clinical pathology, and thirdly, to transform pathology into a social problem requiring institutionalized forms of expertise and treatment for its solution.
>
> (Hepworth 1995: 17)

Those deemed to have failed the test of being 'competent independent adults' are most likely candidates for admission to institutional settings where the process of being seen as a 'less than whole person' takes root, often through forms of infantilization which, as Hockey and James (1993) demonstrate, is a 'natural' response to dependency, and is very frequently observed in residential homes (Hockey 1989).

Deviancy is therefore, in this instance, a devalued status in terms of the dominant value base of our society, and it is here that current debates concerning 'normalization theory' within the disability literature need to be considered, along with the literature on ageism and the position of older people as service users. Normalization, as proposed by Wolfensberger (1972), charts how and why people with disabilities are devalued in society; how labelling is used to reinforce negative perceptions, and leads to further discrimination and prejudice, especially for those living in institutions. The parallels with the analyses of Townsend, Bytheway and Johnson, Hepworth and Hockey and James, discussed above, are clear. However, while it is interesting to note these parallels, what is more important here is Wolfensberger's translation of normalization theory into practical action to reverse processes of devaluation and promote the adoption of 'normalization' as a guiding principle within service delivery. Smith and Brown (1992: 687) outline Wolfensberger's plans for change in this way:

> Central to his thinking, and subsequently to normalization projects, is the imperative to integrate devalued people into the wider society and to ensure they adopt conventional social roles. This is crucial, he claims, if society is to have its social stereotypes about people with disabilities challenged and if people with disabilities themselves are to have opportunities to learn socially valued ways of behaving from 'valued' people and thereby break out of the negative roles to which they have been assigned (Szivos, 1992).
>
> Essentially, this means that people should be enabled to live, work and spend their leisure time in the same places and in the same fashion as non-disabled, ordinary people. The emphasis is on providing environments and activities which most ordinary citizens would want, and on presenting people with disabilities in ways which enhance their dignity and acceptability to others. This approach has seen people being offered services in ordinary houses, in small pseudo-family groups, and has led to an emphasis on helping people find work, use ordinary facilities and draw friends, acquaintances and sometimes advocates from the general public.

Normalization, which is favoured by some care workers, has been influential, particularly within the development of community care services for people with mental health problems, physical disabilities and learning disabilities. Though adopted to a lesser degree with older service users, examples exist where the principles of normalization have been adapted to form a value base to underpin residential care and other services (King's Fund Centre 1986).

However, those who have commented on normalization theory, while remaining sympathetic to its underlying principles, have argued that it remains a theory that is operational at the individual level, and thus fails to tackle the underlying structural causes of the devaluation (Brown and Smith 1989; 1992; Chappell 1992; Smith and Brown 1992). The question as to what and who are the 'valued' people whom the 'devalued' should strive to emulate, is also raised. And the answer has shown that 'valued' people have the characteristics of traditional and powerful groups, such as males, people in employment, white people and those who are not old. We could add to this list those in good health.

Striving to achieve value (or self-valorization) within a society where the dominant values are underpinned by material power entails the recognition of all that has been learnt about powerlessness from, and through, the experience of women and people from minority ethnic groups. The ways in which this knowledge has been utilized to create new understandings of self-worth and value (Smith and Brown 1992: 690) are equally important. With regard to ageing, there is a need to revalue later life as important and developmental and to reassess the terminal phase in life as having a real place in our lives. Within the residential context such analyses of powerlessness are full of tension and become more poignant for a group of predominantly older women cared for by another, largely female, group of care workers (with added dimensions of social class, mental health and/or ethnic differences, in some cases).

Caring: the domestic and the institutional

In 1962, it may have been true that many of the people Townsend talked to in residential homes did not need to be there. The need for residential care homes might then have been challenged in terms of the scant alternative provision of accommodation and care services – but is this still the case? In Chapter 2, we presented evidence which suggested that residential care, while a more common experience among those in their eighties, was still a selective experience. As noted above, Townsend also demonstrated that many residents were unrepresentative of the older population, and he comments: 'in part, institutions emulate, or deputise for, families in providing care for certain elderly people whose family resources are meagre' (Townsend 1981: 18). So the institution is both a form of control and a provider of care. Townsend gave strong support for the family care of older people. He saw residential care as undermining the ability of the family to care and acting as a deterrent against the development of community services which would enable family members to go on caring. Thus, family care is the valued model of care. Townsend (1981: 13–15) suggested that:

- residential care acts as a deterrent and so deters individuals and families from asking for help at times of great stress;
- it is a cheap form of intervention because it is a selective substitute for public housing and community services;
- it has regulated public ideas about how long the family should go on caring.

These comments portray residential care as controlling inasmuch as it both provides a refuge for those older people deemed marginal because of their extreme dependent status and, at the same time, acts as a symbol to deter the family from seeking help from the state. It is from the ambiguity of circumstances such as these that symbols draw their strength and maintain their currency.

Townsend's views are grounded in early work on the family life of older people (Townsend 1957; Rosser and Harris 1965; Willmott and Young, 1957; 1960) which showed the way in which older people's lives were embedded in their family and local community, and which reinforced the value of 'home life' and domestic care. The domestic home has been widely adopted as the valued model on which residential care is based, in terms of not only the physical but also the social psychological environment (Willcocks *et al.* 1987). Yet, because the institutional can never match the domestic there is a conflict between them. In a more recent discussion of caring, Dalley (1993: 110) has this to say about the balance between domestic and institutional care:

The pervading ideology is . . . one which sees caring as primarily a domestic task (and thus a gendered task); this then fuels more generalised attitudes towards informal caring. The 'family-based model of care' (Dalley, 1988) has become the only model of value. Other forms, such as institutional or group forms of care, have been rendered unacceptable, partly because they have failed in terms of their own standards but also because they do not meet ideological norms either. Community care . . . is founded on this principle. 'Dependent' people are best cared for in their own homes, preferably by members of their own families. Failing this, surrogate family forms are deemed to be appropriate . . . Varied forms of care are rendered suitable by being cast in the mould of the family-based model.

The importance of family and informal (i.e. unpaid, unarranged) care for older people is reflected in considerable literary outpouring in the 1980s, including the work of feminist writers concerned with the way 'care in the community' increasingly became equated with 'care by the family' and in the main 'care by women' (Finch and Groves 1980; 1982; 1983; Lewis and Meredith 1988; Qureshi and Walker 1989). The drives behind this research have been varied: the impact of economic retrenchment and the greater emphasis on community care policies; the changing nature of women's employment patterns and patterns of employment/unemployment in general; the growing care needs of the very old; and the ideological dominance of a market economy.

Such research has none the less facilitated the unpicking of the complexities of caring, distinguishing between different components; for instance, between physical tending, emotional support, general concern (see Parker 1981; Graham 1983; Bulmer 1987). It has generated greater understanding of the obligations and commitments which exist between family members (Finch 1989; 1995; Finch and Mason 1992). The extent of the stress (physical, financial, emotional) experienced by care givers and the recognition that they have needs alongside those who receive care (Nissel and Bonnerjea 1982; Charlesworth *et al.* 1984; Pitkeathley 1991) has been revealed in these writings. The tensions which are often present in trying to meet the needs of those who give and receive care in the community have led to calls for alternative forms of services, including alternative residential services (Finch 1984). However, others – particularly from within the disability movement – have argued that in making the carer visible and prominent recipients of care may be further disempowered (Morris, 1991; 1995). There are no easy answers to these tensions, highlighting again the powerlessness of both groups, and while the value of family and home life are being reaffirmed, writers such as Dalley (1993: 123) remind us of the need to rethink forms of accommodation and care.

It is hard to see how these opposing views can be reconciled, although since both groups are disadvantaged by current policies, it would be in both their interests that some sort of reconciliation was reached. Perhaps alternatives to family-based models of care may need to be re-examined. Within the framework of community care policies and the above debates within the disability movement these models have been rejected out of hand. Yet, if . . . informal care itself is often unacceptable – because it imposes too great a burden on women (as carers and care recipients) and because it represents an abdication of collective responsibility – then alternatives may have to be found.

The reality of informal care for older people in the 1980s and 1990s shows that the majority in need of care are helped by family, friends and neighbours. However, while there are millions of people who help with a range of tasks (see Green 1988), those providing intensive personal and physical care form a much smaller group of some 1.4–1.7 million (Parker and Lawton 1990a; 1990b), often being co-resident spouses, both male and female (Arber and Ginn 1990). Thus, those with the heaviest caring responsibilities are often older people themselves, and further work has demonstrated the interdependent nature of caring relationships in old age, with not only the distinction between 'principal care giver' and 'care receiver' becoming blurred but also an increasing recognition of the complex interweaving of informal and formal systems of care inside and outside the domestic setting. For carers, the residential option often ends their responsibilities, abruptly leaving them only with guilt, rather than an opportunity to continue to share care within another place. The opening up of residential care to family and friends is an important aspect of maintaining the value of being part of a family. That families withdraw at this point is symptomatic of both the strength of the institutions and, often, their personal exhaustion.

Care and control

The currency of care is in many senses dependence. We have seen in this chapter the complex interactions between caring and controlling which have characterized residential settings over the years. We have also seen that this relationship may be in the process of being reworked as new ideas and ideologies replace earlier ones associated with control rather than care. But we are also left with the view that if care is to have the ascendancy over control, then the value we place on the end of life needs to be reassessed and the public and private worlds of formal and informal care need to coalesce rather than compete. In Chapter 5 we take these ideas further by considering developments in the form and function of residential care today.

5

Form and function

In characterizing the design philosophy and associated living arrangements for residential care homes, there was a phrase in the professional language of the 1970s and 1980s which points to a degree of confusion and avoidance. Homes were described as aspiring to a form that befits their function, although neither the concept of form nor that of function was necessarily elaborated.

> Much of the evidence ... confirms the view that an adequate rationale for residential care has never been fully developed. The definition in the National Assistance Act, 1948, provides us with a necessary but insufficient explanation for a policy which aims to deliver care in an institutional setting rather than in the community. In a sense, there is a deliberate attempt to offer something that is distinct and separate from the familiar mix of domiciliary support services; yet the explanation for this sharp dichotomy cannot be traced in the policy documents and there is a blurring of the process which might direct a client along route A or route B.
>
> (Willcocks *et al.* 1987: 143)

The admissions lottery

So far we have charted a number of important issues which relate to residential care as we now perceive it. In Chapter 4 we considered the proposition that residential care is a form of more or less benign state control, exercised through the caring symbol of domesticity. The consequence is that residential care, particularly the form it takes and the associated admissions arrangements, functions as a stimulus for families to care for older people at home. In this way the older person who makes the move to residential care can be construed as deviant in at least two ways: first, the family has not been able to respond to his or her needs, nor to do its duty within the domestic setting; and second, the older person has not been able to preserve a degree of choice or social autonomy by remaining at home.

There is evidence that some older people who wish to remain independent of their families and not to place demands upon them, or those who may lack family support altogether, see alternative accommodation and care not as something to dread but as a rational and legitimate alternative to meet their needs as they grow older and, perhaps, less able to manage at home. However, the first choice may not be residential care but something more akin to housing with care, provided as and when necessary. It is important to acknowledge that understandings of caring at home have, in recent years, been augmented through accounts of carers' experiences. The demands on carers can be great and, without adequate community support which is flexible and fits in with the informal system, caring arrangements may break down. Alternatively, they may continue under stress and impose unreasonable costs on committed individuals.

The strains on informal arrangements often surface when an older person is admitted to hospital. Here, as a formal system takes over, family and friends may often feel relief and, for the first time, may be in a position to take stock. But once the crisis has passed, discharge from hospital has to be faced. At this point supported accommodation may seem, to all concerned – sometimes including the older person him or herself – the only tolerable alternative. These decisions, as we saw in Chapter 3, often gain added weight from the medical profession which lends legitimacy on medical grounds – often ignoring the unforeseen social consequences.

The rationale for a move to a residential care home – as opposed to a form of supported housing or a nursing home – may then come down to decisions around home circumstances, care needs, individual determination to move in one direction or another, and financial constraints and possibilities. Decisions about residential care are frequently made in contexts of very limited alternatives – perceived and actual. The interesting question arising out of all of these scenarios is, however, what features and factors would render residential care the chosen alternative, the positive choice.

Moving towards an answer requires a more subtle understanding as to where and how care takes place and just what it consists of – that is, understandings of form and function. More importantly, the question arises as to what older people say they want in terms of accommodation and care, and the mix of these and other elements, such as companionship.

Shifting images of residential care

In terms of both policy and practice, residential care has assumed an image founded upon models of domestic settings and family life (see Willcocks *et al.* 1987). We argued a decade ago that this representation has been used, consciously and unconsciously, to dissociate residential care from the controlling and negative images associated with institutions. At the same time, formal residential care has been scaled down to the level of the individual. A person-centred approach to practice aims to break down the depersonalization which can accompany 'batch-living'. Thus, in principle, residential care has attempted to move itself ever closer to a form of accommodation and care within the community (NISW 1988a) .

Recognition has also been given to the two worlds of residential care – the living and working environments which must coexist, where older people are cared for by those other than their relatives or friends, and which thus require systems of accountability and mechanisms for regulation. Arbitrary boundaries and uncomfortable relationships still exist between life in the community and life in a home. Accordingly, major interventions in the social, physical and ideological fabric of residential living have tended to be marked by changes in form or appearance rather than by challenges to function or shifts in the fundamental meanings which attach to residential living where older people are concerned.

Ambiguity about residential care persists. The public debate which took place about the future development of community care services throughout the 1980s was intended to place a brake on the continued expansion of residential care. This was a key issue, primarily because of financial concerns (Audit Commission 1985; 1986; Griffiths 1988), but also because the family/domestic model was brought to the fore. The role of residential care, and the context that permits or requires homes to function at all, was sidelined as a negative issue. Yet, as contended in Chapter 4, there are compelling reasons for, and there is plenty of material to fuel, such a debate. In this chapter we want to explore the role of residential care in the 1990s, placing it alongside developments in housing, social and health care for older people.

The contexts of caring

A range of settings can be identified in which the delivery of health and social care services to older people, generally over 80 years of age, can take place – the domestic home, day centre, family placement scheme, residential care home, nursing home, continuing care ward. Each setting is made up of – and takes its character from – a mix of the physical environment and social relationships between people, some of which are founded in a particular professional practice. In Chapter 2 we considered some of the facts about the people and places which make up residential care and we acknowledged that residential care provides a service for a minority of older people. The majority of older people in need of care are living at home and may be receiving support from family and friends; however, they may not be in receipt of services or help at all – either formal or informal.

Most care received by older people at home is provided by those who do not live with them – it is extra-resident care. However, where care is co-resident the help provided is likely to be more intense and offered for longer periods of time. It is also more likely to be provided by a spouse (Arber and Ginn 1990). Differences in longevity mean that the living arrangements of older men and women vary considerably. Three-quarters of older men live in their own homes, a majority with their spouse. Yet, while men may commonly be cared for by a spouse, a substantial proportion of older spouse carers are men. Older women, on the other hand are more likely to live in a range

Figure 5.1   Facts about care at home

- For older people living in their own homes most care is provided by the family – both practical and emotional support.
- Most informal care is extra-resident rather than co-resident.
- Three-quarters of older men live in their own home, a majority with their spouse.
- Older women live in a variety of domestic settings: alone (almost half); with spouse; in their own home with others; and with adult children in circumstances where they are not the householder.
- Older people in receipt of community nursing, home care, meals services or occupational therapy services are most likely to live alone, be over 80 years of age, be house-bound, score high on measures of disability, live without standard amenities and have a dementing condition.
- Older people who receive day care or respite care are most likely to live alone, be over 80 years of age, score high on measures of disability, be thought to be 'at risk' of residential care, have mental health problems, need help with washing and bathing and be more likely to have a carer who is a child rather than spouse.

Sources: Sinclair and Williams (1990); Sinclair *et al.* (1990); Twigg *et al.* (1990); Arber and Ginn (1991); Allen *et al.* (1992); McCafferty (1994).

of domestic settings: almost half live on their own; others live with their husband, or in their own home with others, and a proportion have moved in with an adult child. Figure 5.1 summarizes some of these arrangements and shows that those in receipt of formal services at home or at day settings are usually living alone, over 80 years of age, and coping with severe mental or physical disabilities.

Since the late 1980s we have also been aware of the targeting and rationing of community care services to older people (Allen *et al.* 1992; Wistow 1995). The NHS and Community Care Act is based on a needs-led rather than a resource-led model of care, yet evidence suggests that services provided through public sector budgets are constrained and targeted on an ever smaller group of people who are seen as most in need (Hoyes *et al.* 1994; Marchant 1995). Limits placed on the provision of community services are felt most strongly by those who do not have private resources to service their own needs and provide choice. Hence, the domestic environment as a caring environment may also become constrained with ever greater pressure being put on informal carers and the resources of the family. The question may then be posed as to whether the domestic environment of a house-bound older person with limited resources may become as controlling as an institutional setting (see Gavilan 1990). If this is the case, then will it affect the preferences of older people which, as we have noted, have to date been to remain in their

Figure 5.2 Proposed hierarchy of elderly person's preference for caring contexts

A. In elderly person's own home – self-care.
B. In elderly person's own home – care provided by co-resident:
    (i)   spouse;
    (ii)   other same-generation relative;
    (iii)   child or non-kin.
C. In elderly person's own home – care provided by extra-resident:
    (iv)   child;
    (v)   other relative;
    (vi)   neighbour, friend or volunteer.
D. In care giver's own home – care provided by co-resident:
    (vii) unmarried child;
    (viii) married child.

Source: Arber and Ginn (1991: 144, Fig. 8.2).

own home. The question for the older person and the carer is whether personal control over meaningful space is such that restrictions are to be endured.

Arber and Ginn (1991) propose a hierarchy of elderly people's preferences for caring contexts in the community (see Figure 5.2). They argue that older women are 'disadvantaged in being less likely to receive care in circumstances which allow them to preserve their sense of independence and control over their lives' (Arber and Ginn 1991: 140). This conclusion is based on a review of the survey evidence of the circumstances of older people living at home. Within their proposed hierarchy, Arber and Ginn (1991: 143) also argue that formal services can provide 'an enabling role in any of the caring contexts, and in so doing may prevent the frail elderly person entering a less preferential caring context'.

However, there is evidence that community services may not always be experienced as life-enhancing, even if they do prevent a move and are life-sustaining. Certainly, older women are most likely to feel the loss of role when they have to receive care at home, and they are most likely to live in supported environments. But we still know very little about the feelings of those older people at the receiving end of care provision, about their lives in various settings, or their experience of a range of care options. A 1994–5 study of 100 recipients of care showed that the structures of care delivery are not well aligned with the ways users see the structures of their own lives at home (Kellaher, forthcoming), a finding which is echoed by Morris (1995) for the experiences of women with disabilities as care receivers.

A number of services – such as respite care, day care and day hospital care – remove the older person from his or her domestic setting for part of the day or for weeks at a time. If this occurs on a regular basis, then not only may care become shared between informal and formal carers, but also the older person experiences a regular, and potentially stimulating though sometimes disorientating, change of environment. In many cases such a mix of services is offered in order to provide respite for a carer, and in some instances there is the explicit intention of easing the transition from home care to residential or nursing home care. However, examples are also seen of respite being offered to older people living alone in order to extend their lives at home.

Caring in a supported place

Of course, some older people have already chosen to move from 'ordinary' housing into a more specialized housing form and they are more likely to have done so, initially, for reasons of housing need rather than care needs. The Department of the Environment (DoE) survey of 'subsidized specialized social housing' (i.e. to rent) for older people records that in 1991 there were 641,765 units of accommodation – 51 per cent being sheltered housing units with a warden and communal facilities (see Figure 5.3). The largest providers of subsidized specialist housing are local housing authorities (73 per cent of all units in England in 1991), followed by housing associations (23 per cent), with the remainder being provided by the Abbeyfield society (1 per cent) and almshouses (3 per cent) (McCafferty 1994). In addition, there is specialized housing for sale. In 1990 it was estimated that around 80,000 older people were living in such accommodation, although Rolfe *et al.* (1993) report that in recent years sales have been in decline, along with trends in the housing market generally.

The range of specialized housing for older people includes bungalows, flats and maisonettes. The DoE report adopts the traditional classification of sheltered housing types to describe the subsidized stock in 1988 (see Figure 5.3). This includes a small percentage of alternative housing such as granny flats or Abbeyfield supported housing. The origins of these alternative forms of shared living differ from those of sheltered housing and we return to these differences. The history of sheltered housing since the 1950s highlights its origins as part of a housing policy initiated at that time to address social aspects of accommodation and, at the same time, to encourage the release of what was seen as under-occupied family-sized housing. In other words, there were both push and pull factors which influenced the development of local authority sheltered housing as a bricks-and-mortar response to need (Means 1991).

Inevitably, the concern among providers has changed over the years. Today, older people moving into sheltered accommodation may see this as a final move, and providers seem more willing to confront the consequences and obligations implied by offering a 'home for life' (National Federation of Housing Associations 1993). There has been some criticism from housing organizations that the DoE, in utilizing what are now possibly dated categories to describe this provision, is failing to recognize the growing trend towards harmonizing housing across the accommodation and care spectrum (Roose 1996). This has led to a number of developments: the growth of 'extra care housing', the debate over the role of the warden in sheltered units, the growing diversity of arrangements for providing care within housing units and the recognition that, given appropriate support, older people with a range of mental and physical frailties may continue to live in settings which are

Figure 5.3   Older people living in subsidized specialized social housing, March 1990

Category 1 accommodation
contains specially designed units of accommodation for elderly people of the more active kind. Communal facilities such as a common room, a laundry room or a guest room may also be provided, although these are optional (126,863 units, 20 per cent).

Category 1.5 accommodation*
is broadly similar to category 1 housing but it must have an alarm system and warden support. No communal facilities are provided in this form of accommodation (150,715 units, 23 per cent).

Category 2 accommodation*
consists of schemes with units of accommodation for less active elderly people. They must have a resident or non-resident warden and a system for calling him or her. Communal facilities such as a common room, a laundry room or a guest room must also be provided (328,746 units, 51 per cent).

Category 2.5 accommodation*
consists of what are also known as either 'very sheltered' or 'extra-care' schemes. They are for frail elderly people and have more provision or a greater level of care than category 2 schemes. They may, for example, provide meals, extra wardens, care assistants and additional communal facilities such as special bathrooms, sluice rooms etc. (14,782 units, 2 per cent).

Other specialized housing
Abbeyfield housing, shared/group homes, granny annexes, supportive houses etc. (20,659 units, 3 per cent).

* Category 1.5, 2 and 2.5 accommodation can be grouped as sheltered housing under the definition provided in Schedule 5, paragraph 10 of the 1985 Housing Act.
Source: adapted from McCafferty (1994: 34–6). Crown copyright is reproduced with the permission of the Controller of HMSO.

---

classified and perceived as housing rather than residential (Oldman 1990; McCafferty 1994; Kitwood *et al.* 1995; Lloyd and Austin Locke 1995).

We highlight the various contexts for care in order that the issues surrounding the role of residential care may be put into perspective. The last decade has seen a decline in the number of long-stay hospital beds, and a growth in the number of nursing home places, special units for older people with mental health problems and sheltered housing units. At the same time, the growth in residential care places has slowed down, while those living at home are experiencing the consequences of increased pressures on community services. These trends raise a number of questions about the setting in which care is delivered and the type of care which is needed. Once again, we are reminded of the questions posed by Townsend (1962). Is residential care necessary, and what function does it serve? Do we need more sheltered housing, and housing with care; or do we need more nursing home places rather than residential care homes? Importantly, do older people just want better access to smaller units of ordinary housing integrated within the community and access to properly funded community-based services?

Form: the physical environment

> They seem to think that as we get older they can put us into smaller and smaller accommodation until they finally get us into a coffin.
> (Women's Design Service 1991: 1)

The literature on the meaning of home has shown how important home is for the maintenance of self-identity and personal integrity in later life (see Sixsmith and Sixsmith 1990; Rubenstein and Parmelee 1992; Peace and Holland 1994). The home environment and its surroundings have meanings and memories invested in them, hence a combination of particular physical, social and metaphysical properties which older people struggle to preserve in their environment.

However, as people grow older, they may experience 'environmental press', where their ability to cope with life at home may not be environmentally supported and where the positive aspects of staying put fail to compensate for declining capacities. Of course, in many instances the immediate physical environment may be adapted – a bed may be brought downstairs or a stair lift can be installed. But there are other circumstances where such environmental press operates at a psychological or social level and may influence internal or external features of living at home. In some cases, these inhibiting or restrictive circumstances are managed – with varying degrees of discomfort or distress; in other cases, being unmanageable, they will precipitate a change in accommodation.

The ability to improve the environment, or change accommodation, depends on a number of factors including personal capability; personal orientation to change; family resources and financial resources. In a study by the Women's Design Service (1991) on designing housing for older women, recommendations were made on issues of affordability, mobility and disability; health and support services; caring and design; comfort; safety; security; domestic violence and harassment; and public and private space. It is pertinent that 'affordability' was placed at the head of this list, and the first recommendation is that 'more housing choices for women with low incomes need to be provided' (Women's Design Service 1991: 58).

Here we return to the concerns of the majority of older people on low incomes, for without choice over accommodation decisions are often deferred. And for the many older women who face these decisions alone the issue may not only be one of limited income, but also of confidence in dealing with matters of housing finance (Peace 1993b). Deferred decisions about 'ordinary housing' may ultimately lead to a move at a later stage, either to live with children or into residential or nursing home care.

Personal space and shared living

When asked about the design of accommodation, the older women interviewed in the Women's Design Service (1991) study commented on a wide range of issues. These included specific design features to assist those with disabilities and those who had to perform caring tasks; the balance of personal and communal space; the ability to remain mobile in the community; and issues of personal safety; and the development of communal settings alternative to residential care. Their conception of environment was broadly based and predicated on the integration of home and community. Their comments on design acknowledged their own needs as people who may require a 'prosthetic' environment to support them while remaining a part of a wider community. They had not written themselves off as people to be placed apart from the community.

The views of these women may be considered alongside those of the older people who took part in the National Consumer Study of Local Authority Old People's Homes undertaken by the present authors in 1980–1. The main aim of this study was to enable older residents to talk about the physical environment of residential homes and, thereby, to inform a revision of the then current Building Note on residential accommodation (DHSS and Welsh Office 1973).

This research remains the only major national study of residential care to ask residents detailed questions about the physical environment in which they lived. To summarize, residents' responses showed how important it was for them to live in residential settings which the researchers categorized as 'the normal, the unexceptional and the non-institutional' (Willcocks *et al.* 1987: 145). The responses were construed as a challenge to 'the conventional wisdom of policy-makers, choosing a lifestyle that reflects as far as possible the everyday taken-for-granted aspects of living in the community' (Willcocks *et al.* 1987: 149).

In this way, we interpreted residents' comments as giving support to the model of community living based on the tradition of a family home as they knew it. In particular, the data reinforced the importance of private space and the need for individuals to have the right to determine their own life-style as best they could, within a balance of public and private settings in the home.

A contemporary review of these data shows that in the past we had not fully accounted for the gendered nature of domestic space. For women, in particular, there is a significant social distance between living at home in a domestic setting and living in a home that is communal. This might suggest that we need to encourage a more sustained and creative search for new models of shared living.

The residential flatlet

The residents cohort of 1981 helped us to construct a new vision of the residential home, reported first in 1982, and throughout a series of publications in the early and mid-1980s culminating in *Private Lives in Public Places* in 1987 (see Willcocks *et al.* 1982; 1987; Peace *et al.* 1982; Kellaher *et al.* 1985). The

Figure 5.4   The residential flatlet
Source: Willcocks *et al.* (1987: 150).

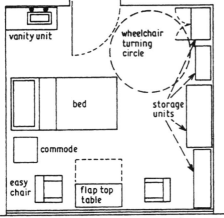

sketch layout of resident's living room (15 m² approx.)

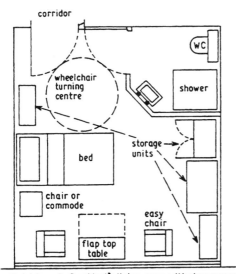

sketch layout of resident's living-room with shower room
and WC en suite (18m² approx.)

major focus of the new residential design was the residential flatlet (see Figure 5.4) described as follows:

> It would constitute a larger and more flexible version of the existing single room, different from sheltered housing insofar as it would remain part of an essentially supportive environment. Yet the residential flatlet

would offer unmistakable personal territory, lockable from the inside, and within it the resident would be firmly in control of everyday routine . . .

This flatlet should be large enough to accommodate some personal items of substantial furniture such as a bed or a sideboard which might evoke significant memories and affirm individual status and identity . . . It is not envisaged that this room would contain elaborate cooking facilities; main catering would be undertaken centrally but meals could be taken and shared with neighbours or visitors in the individual flatlets . . . a range of support services would then be built around the flatlet; sanitary services such as a vanity unit would form an integral part of the flatlet, or be located adjacent to it, as would the shower plus WC. Baths would be provided separately. Two levels of catering would be necessary to offer centrally prepared and served meals for those who chose to be served, and self-catering in a kitchenette for those who chose to help themselves . . . At least one large lounge must also be offered, possibly incorporating part of the entrance hall, as an alternative meeting place . . . In addition, homes must be designed to incorporate key features which promote familiarity and trigger orientation within the macro environment. Basic design features should assist residents to recognise the shape of the whole building, thus rendering the physical world comprehensible.

(Willcocks, *et al.* 1987: 149–51)

The model of an institution built around residential flatlets was a design solution which sought to bring the views of the older 'consumer' to bear on both new building and the adaptation of existing buildings. It was underpinned by a philosophy which recognized the primacy of past lives and settings, the maintenance of skills and activity, of community links and personal relationships, and advocated greater sharing of care and responsibility between formal and informal carers (Willcocks *et al.* 1987: 140–59). Thus, residents were to be recognized as 'real people' with 'real lives', and this opening up of the institution would encourage community integration and provide a check on any tendency towards inwardness and abuse.

While the home would offer grouped living arrangements, the emphasis would be on the individual within his or her own personal space, rather than on the model of small 'family' group living in residential care which had been advocated in the 1973 Building Note (DHSS and Welsh Office 1973). The form or design of the accommodation would facilitate individual control but would not be deterministic. It would, moreover, cope with a resident population that would be increasingly differentiated by age, health status, gender and ethnicity.

This research and its published findings were circulating during a period of great change for the residential sector. The early to mid-1980s saw the striking expansion of the private homes sector . Many homes were small in scale and resulted from the adaptation of large domestic houses. As CESSA's research in 1985 showed, the early phase of adaptation raised particular issues regarding shared personal space and reduced space for aspects of communal

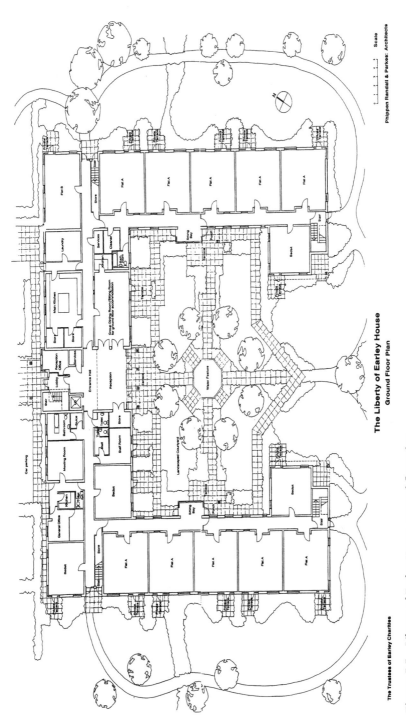

The Liberty of Earley House
Ground Floor Plan

Phippen Randall & Parkes: Architects

Figure 5.5 Liberty of Earley House, ground floor plan
Source: Reproduced with the kind permission of Phippen Randall & Parkes, architects.

living (Weaver *et al.* 1985). Yet where there was capital for new build, there has been a move in the direction of constructing the residential flatlet model. The floor plan in Figure 5.5 is for a housing scheme that is registered as a residential care home, and which won the new build category within the Care Homes Design Awards in 1995. It is based on a mix of one-bedroom flats and bedsitting units with additional communal dining rooms, bathing facilities and shared laundry.

Sheltered housing in transition

At the time of writing *Private Lives in Public Spaces*, it was suggested that the residential flatlet model was firmly rooted in the residential sector, 'different from sheltered housing insofar as it would remain part of an essentially supportive environment' (Willcocks *et al.* 1987: 149).

But more recent developments in very sheltered housing have direct parallels with our earlier recommendations. The recent DoE study of subsidized specialized housing mentioned above shows that three-fifths of the units are self-contained flats, a third are bungalows and, of the remainder, non-self-contained flats dominate (McCafferty 1994: 42). When this material is analysed by category of accommodation, it shows that while most ordinary and very sheltered housing (categories 2, 2.5) is made up of self-contained flats, 32 per cent of very sheltered housing is in the form of non-self-contained flats (McCafferty 1994: 43, Table 2.7). Nearly half of all units in categories 1 and 1.5 are bungalows.

The study also shows that there is variation according to provider. Almost all local authority very sheltered housing units are self-contained flats, while nearly a half of housing association stock of this type is in the form of non-self-contained flats. This distinction between self- and non-self-containment is important when comparing developments in specialized housing with that of residential care and the proposed residential flatlet model outlined above. The concept of 'non-self-containment' indicates that certain facilities concerning bathing or cooking do not form an integral part of the individual's accommodation; they are offered communally. In essence, then, the residential flatlet model is very similar to the current design for some very sheltered housing.

The difference in design between local authority and housing association accommodation is explained by McCafferty (1994) in terms of a range of factors; in particular, there is a strong influence exerted by the availability of financial subsidies and regulation:

> This difference may be due to several factors, such as the influence of capital and revenue funding regimes encouraging non self-contained dwellings and the requirements of registration as residential care homes. It is not likely to be due to differences in the frailty of local authority and housing association residents.
>
> (McCafferty 1994: 43)

Differences between ordinary sheltered housing and very sheltered housing are also seen in terms of the size of units. One-bedroom units are most common across all categories of provision; indeed, as 'the frailty of the intended resident increases so the size of units decreases' (McCafferty 1994: 44). The comments made earlier ring true.

Something akin to 'bedsits' is most common in very sheltered housing, particularly that owned by housing associations. This trend, however, may be changing for it is also noted that within the planned provision of very sheltered housing more self-contained accommodation is likely (McCafferty 1994: 120) and this is said to be more 'in line with residents' own preferences' (cf. Tinker 1989: para. 13). Future provision is also more likely to be met by housing associations than local authorities, changing the balance of providers. With all these shifts, very sheltered housing is now being seen as a real alternative to residential care, as this comment from the Wagner report indicates:

> In practice, very sheltered housing can provide frail elderly residents with a level of care equivalent to that given by the traditional residential home, combined with a greater degree of continued privacy and independence than the latter can usually offer.
>
> (NISW 1988a: 21)

Alternative specialized housing

Bedsit provision plus communal facilities are also found in the shared housing referred to as 'other specialized housing' above. However, it is important to separate this provision from the other forms of sheltered housing. Shared or group housing such as that provided by the Abbeyfield society has been developed within a particular philosophical tradition of communal living which specifically mentions companionship. As Cooper *et al.* (1994: 18) record in a study of shared housing, this form of living arrangement has usually been deliberately chosen by those residents who value what the researchers call 'integrative security': 'this form of housing enabled residents to be on their own, but never alone in the way some felt they would be in self-contained accommodation'. These same residents expressed a desire to remain independent of their families, and to relinquish some of the responsibilities of domestic life. The authors suggest that shared housing such as that provided by Abbeyfield offers a valuable alternative form of environment, with a distinctive function which will suit a specific group of people. Indeed, it is a housing form which attracts a very small sub-group of predominantly older women who have previously owned their own homes or rented privately. The authors go on to indicate that the increasing tendency to emphasize independent living within private space and the funding of self-contained housing through Housing Corporation 'special needs' funding has led to a change in the ways these forms of shared housing are viewed. This may make it a somewhat vulnerable form in the future: 'The image of shared housing has . . . suffered from the declining importance attached to the idea of communality and the growing emphasis on independent living and personal autonomy as the central goal of supported housing' (Cooper *et al.* 1994: 3).

The issues surrounding specialized housing are therefore to be found at various levels. There is a difference in philosophy between shared living which stresses degrees of communality (as in the Abbeyfield model) and models which stress the importance of independent living. There is a difference of scale/resources between the needs of the care industries for economies of scale as costs rise, and the need to meet the preferences of the majority of consumers for private space and the right to control and organize their own life-style (Cooper *et al.* 1994). And there is a difference in ideology between those who have challenged 'special needs' housing (in the same way in which Townsend and others have attacked residential care), seeing it as stigmatizing, segregating and failing to address the real issues of poverty, access to ordinary housing and to community services (Middleton 1987; Arnold *et al.* 1993); and others who support a diversity of provision (Watson and Cooper 1992; Cooper *et al.* 1994).

Returning to the discussion about the future form and function of residential care, what is most apparent is that very sheltered housing and some forms of shared living arrangements occupy similar territory in terms of design features to that of the most recent purpose-built residential care homes. Indeed, some very sheltered and special schemes are registered under the Registered Homes Act 1984 (Sealy 1995).

Registration places demands on providers to meet standards concerning the physical environment. The emphasis has been placed on providing people with private space and activity space. *Home Life*, the 1984 code of practice which, while not mandatory, has been extremely influential in setting standards, recommended single rooms for people who needed long term-care: 'It is highly desirable that all residents in long-term care should have their own room (unless they prefer otherwise), as well as the use of communal areas' (CPA 1984: 23). In *A Better Home Life* (CPA 1996) these principles are reinforced, along with an acknowledgement that the provision of single rooms has implications for cost, size and access. Nevertheless, the proportion of single rooms in a home has become one of the central indicators, if not symbols, of quality in relation to the physical environment.

Nursing homes in transition

Comparisons can also be made between residential care homes and nursing homes. As we saw in Chapter 2, the independent nursing home sector has grown rapidly in recent years and there has been a greater emphasis on new build than in the residential sector. However, whether purpose-built or adapted, one of the key issues as we move further along the social – medical continuum becomes one of surveillance and the professional need to monitor those in need of nursing care. Can these needs be met outside the hospital setting? The answer in terms of design is a confident 'yes'. Bond and Bond (1989) give a striking example of what can be done, in their evaluation of the three national health nursing homes for older people set up as an experiment in the 1980s. Here, three nursing homes were adapted from existing buildings (originally a farm, a maternity home and a hotel). These were set alongside six long-stay units for older people. In Figures 5.6 and 5.7, floor plans for

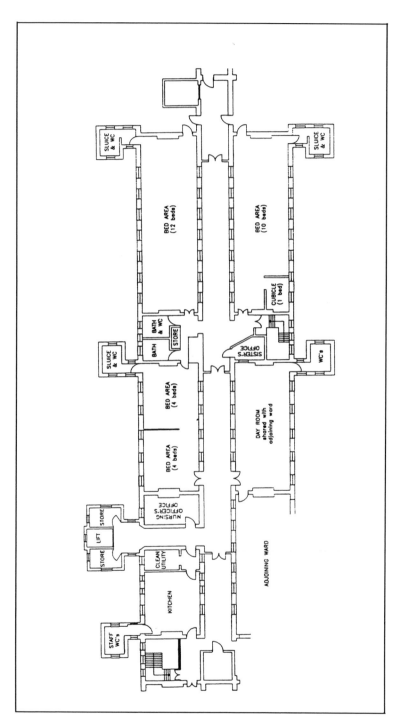

Figure 5.6 Hospital ward for older people, part of a former workhouse building which has been absorbed into a department of geriatric medicine

Source: Case-study location from Bond and Bond (1989: Figure 3.2.1).

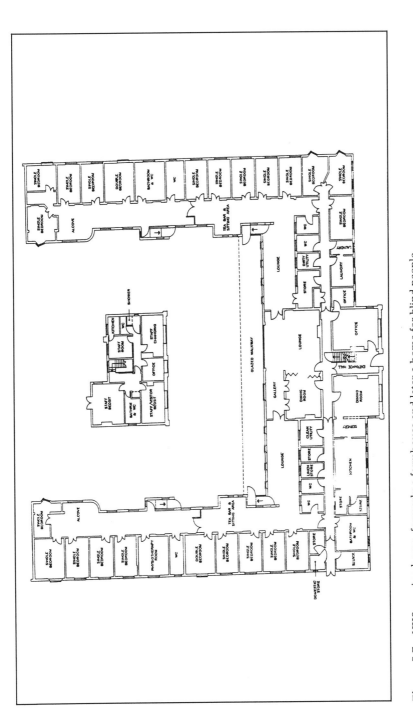

Figure 5.7 NHS nursing home, formerly a farmhouse and later a home for blind people
Source: Case-study location from Bond and Bond (1989: Figure 3.28).

a hospital setting and for one of the experimental nursing homes are shown. As Bond and Bond (1989) point out, while nursing home conversion is still far from ideal, there are benefits in terms of personal space, privacy for intimate personal treatment, shorter distances between facilities, and a more comfortable and stimulating design. As a separate entity, the nursing home takes on a life of its own. No longer are residents/patients and staff part of a relatively impersonal organization.

Special schemes for special groups

Over the last decade, the move to create small-scale, domestic-type accommodation has also occurred in a number of special schemes developed especially for older people who suffer dementia of one kind or another (Marshall 1993; Dunlop 1994). While such schemes form only a very small proportion of the non-domestic accommodation for this group, they provide models of what is seen as good practice in design. For someone with imperfect memory, scale and size are thought to be important. A small scale, of between 8 and 12 people, is believed to provide an environment which does not overstimulate in terms of people, noise and activity. The need to comprehend space easily through visual clues, and to feel secure while being able to move about with some confidence, is also seen to be important and to affect reactions to scale. In the Lewisham and North Southwark Health Authority, these design principles have been put into effect through the development of the Domus programme of small residential nursing homes, using a housing model of care. They are facilities operated in partnership between a housing association and the health service (see Murphy *et al.* 1994). Here, the design of the Domus is just one part of an overall philosophy which sees every resident as a 'citizen tenant' (Murphy and Macdonald 1994). The development of the first and subsequent designs was described as follows:

> The first Domus at Churchdown was designed by Jane Lind of Jane Lind Associates, a small independent practice based at Wadsworth in Sussex. Tenders for the construction were sought in 1987 when the property boom was still in progress and before the sharp fall in both land prices and building costs between 1990 and 1993. The cost limits the health authority had to work to were very out of date and no automatic index was available to take account of the subsequent rise of prices. Costs were, therefore, very tightly controlled and a number of desirable features had to be omitted. Good standards were nevertheless achieved: 11 m² bedrooms, a spacious living room and dining room and two other sitting areas around the building. Because of the wish to make the building as unlike a hospital as possible, a nurses station was not included and a staff room was also omitted. This was partly to make it as homelike as possible for the residents, although pragmatic cost reasons probably played a part in the decision.
>
> The building design was a considerable success and won praise from both relatives and the staff who were employed. The Domus very soon generated a relaxed and homelike atmosphere and fulfilled the association's expectations . . .
>
> The main lesson learnt from the first scheme was the necessity to give

thought to the needs of those who will be working at the Domus. It is arguable that the inclusion of a properly designed and thought out nurses station – rather than a spare corner of the landing as became necessary at 1 Churchdown – and of a staff room and staff lockers, detracts from the Domus as a place of residence. The feeling of ownership by the residents can still be emphasised without making life uncomfortable for staff, and the subsequent two Domuses have both included better staff amenities. Ownership is emphasised through different colour schemes in each room and the use and decoration of the common rooms and corridors. It has proved possible to include staff facilities without them seeming intrusive or making the later buildings feel like hospitals.

(Bendle 1994: 20–1)

Here the delicate balance which has to be achieved between domestic lives and working lives was recognized, and a compromise appears to be realizable.

All of these examples of different forms of living show a degree of consensus around the need for manageable personal space; but they also reveal tensions around communality in daily living and the need for variety; and around economies of scale. They also leave unresolved the impact of changing forms of accountability and regulation on the physical and social environment. The emphasis on providing individual living space with its roots in ordinary domestic lives in ordinary domestic housing, does not translate easily to the special setting without increasing the scale, size and complexity of the building. It can be argued, then, that the residential flatlet model, while rooted legitimately in the views of residents, has limitations. It may embody older people's desire to remain in ordinary housing, but it does not necessarily carry domestic values and traditions into an alternative setting. Part of the difficulty is that accommodation forms only part of the picture, and to explore these issues further we must pursue the question of function for these buildings. This, in turn, brings us to the heart of the matter – supportive services and the care offered to residents.

The boundaries of residential care

The boundaries of residential care were of central concern to the Wagner committee when it deliberated in 1987 and 1988 about the future of residential care. It focused on the link between accommodation and care, and it took on board the concern of many groups (such as the National Federation of Housing Associations, MIND and the Campaign for Mentally Handicapped People) that the traditional definitions of residential care were too narrow, failing to recognize an ever wider variety of needs and provision. The separation of accommodation and services also focuses attention on what we mean by services and how they can be delivered.

Again, the Wagner report listed what its authors saw as the needs which could be met through personal social services:

- practical assistance in daily living; this includes the provision of food, warmth, clothing, environmental supports and assistance with personal care like washing, dressing, bathing and going to the toilet.

- practical advice and help in coping with day-to-day problems, and counselling when needed.
- specific teaching and guidance in order to acquire new abilities and skills or to reinforce existing ones . . .
- specialised programmes of care, assessment, treatment and rehabilitation, which aim to produce substantial changes in individuals' functioning so that they can live more freely, independently and with integrity.
- control and containment, but only in the interests of child care or where individuals are at risk of endangering themselves and others.

(NISW 1988a: 21–2)

It argued that 'none of these categories of need requires as a necessary condition that the individual be placed in a special setting in order to receive the services indicated' (NISW 1988a: 22).

The Wagner committee did discuss some circumstances where the delivery of services, as part of an integrated programme of accommodation plus care, may be necessary; but it reinforced the view that all people have a right to 'have access to the full range of community support services which they would have received had they still been living in their own homes' (NISW 1988a: 22).

This separation of accommodation and care is a radical departure from traditional ways of considering residential care, and sits uneasily alongside the requirements of both the National Assistance Act 1948 and the Registered Homes Act 1984, both of which see accommodation and care as inextricably linked.

The National Assistance Act 1948 placed a duty upon local authorities to provide 'residential accommodation for persons who by reason of age, infirmity or any other circumstances are in need of care and attention which is not otherwise available to them' (quoted in Townsend 1962: 33). This all-embracing and much quoted duty has dominated discussion about the function of residential care homes, particularly the phrase 'care and attention'. It creates ambiguity over the definition of personal care as opposed to nursing care, and has triggered numerous attempts to try and distinguish between them (see, for example, DHSS and Welsh Office 1982). The duty defined by the National Assistance Act 1948 has been passed down through successive legislation with the latest attempt at clarification being seen in the Registered Homes Act 1984. As we have seen, the Registered Homes Act 1984 sets out the regulatory framework for the registration and inspection of independent sector provision. It applies to a range of settings which have in common the fact that they provide a place of residence, that is, 'they are places where people spend a period of time in residence, that is to say, they sleep in and receive meals on the premises' (DoH and Welsh Office 1990: 2).

But the Act places a different emphasis on actual residence within its two parts and the type of care provided. Part I states that it concerns 'residential accommodation with both board and personal care for persons in need of personal care'. Whereas Part II of the Act, which covers a range of clinical and non-residential settings, concerns 'premises used . . . for the reception of, and provision of nursing for, persons suffering from any sickness, injury or infirmity' (DoH and Welsh Office 1990: 2).

The distinction is made between personal and nursing care, and, where residential care homes and nursing homes are concerned, the distinguishing criterion is the extent to which the occupants require the kind of attention which falls within the practice of the nursing or medical professions. However, there is continuing ambiguity concerning the commonly used term 'health-related needs' which, in later life, may be associated with long-standing or fluctuating health conditions rather than acute episodes of sickness. The 1984 Act does not provide a comprehensive definition of personal care, though it does state that it may include 'assistance with bodily functions' but not necessarily so. Given this guidance, the National Federation of Housing Associations (NFHA 1987: 14) commented:

> What this probably means is that schemes in which residents are helped with, for example, dressing and washing should not be treated as nursing homes but should be registered as residential care homes.

It went on to quote DHSS guidance notes:

> Residential homes are primarily a means of providing a greater degree of support for those elderly people no longer able to cope with the practicalities of living in their homes even with the help of domiciliary services. The care provided is limited to that appropriate to a residential setting and is broadly equivalent to what might be provided by a competent and caring relative able to respond to emotional as well as physical needs. It includes, for instance, help with washing, bathing, dressing; assistance with toilet needs; the administration of medicines and when a resident falls sick, the kind of attention someone would receive in his own home from a caring relative under guidance of the general practitioner or nurse member of the primary health care team. However, staff of a home are not expected to provide the professional kind of health care that is properly the function of the primary health care services. Nor should residential homes be used as nursing homes or extensions of hospitals.
>
> (NFHA 1987: 14–15)

But has this definition, like the sheltered housing categories, also become obsolete? Has reliance on primary health care services run its course, or is it alive and well? The debate as to what constitutes the boundary between nursing care and personal care is an ongoing one and relates both to the balance between professional traditions and the needs of individuals. In terms of regulation and the imposition of standards (which affect the quality of life of individuals), the designation of registration as either a residential care home or a nursing home will be crucial. Thus, staff in residential care homes are required by the Residential Care Homes Regulations (1984) to be 'suitably qualified and competent', while within nursing homes The Nursing Homes and Mental Nursing Homes Regulations (1984) require that they 'provide adequate professional, technical, ancillary and other staff in relation to the size and type of establishment'. The person in charge of a nursing home must be a registered medical practitioner or a first-level registered nurse. The registering authority sets minimum staffing levels for each nursing home as a condition of registration, and a record is kept of the qualifications and grades of staff (O'Kell 1995; CPA 1996) – though it appears that one nurse on duty at any one time is a common practice (Royal College of Nursing 1992).

Such conditions have important implications for environment and staffing and, consequently, for the financial costs to residents. Establishing the necessary mix of skills (trained and untrained) for the staff body is therefore a current issue. Some argue that few nursing home residents need 24-hour care, although they may need 24-hour nursing management (O'Kell 1995: 15); while others fiercely protect professional divisions against what may be seen as cost-cutting measures. Dual registration of homes may overcome some of these staffing problems, but at present there are several bureaucratic and other issues to be considered as a consequence of dual status.

Some forms of very sheltered housing operated by housing associations and by Abbeyfield are now registered under the Act. One immediate consequence of the regulatory framework is demonstrated in the DoE study, *Living Independently*, which indicates that higher staffing ratios imposed through registration can dramatically increase running costs (McCafferty, 1994: 7).

Continuing care

During the mid 1990s we have also seen an attempt by the NHS and the local authorities to clarify the position concerning the provision of continuing care for older people (DoH 1995a; Age Concern 1995a). As discussed in Chapter 2, this issue arose in the context of the failure by some health authorities to meet their obligations to older patients particularly in relation to long-stay in-patient care. The guidance issued by the DoH in February 1995 states that the NHS is:

responsible for arranging and funding a range of services to meet the needs of people who require continuing physical and mental health care ... including:

- continuing in-patient care under specialist supervision in hospital or in a nursing home;
- specialist health care support to people in nursing homes or residential care homes or the community;
- community health services to people at home or in residential care homes.

(DoH 1995a: 6)

Accordingly, the role of specialist and community health services in providing for older people, in whichever setting they may live, has been reinforced. At the same time, a new category – continuing in-patient care – has been added to the accepted range of options. Such care may be provided either in NHS hospitals or in nursing homes and is defined as being necessary for people:

- where the complexity or intensity of their medical, nursing care or other clinical care or the need for frequent not easily predictable interventions requires the regular (in the majority of cases this might be weekly or more frequent) supervision of a consultant, specialist nurse or other NHS member of the multidisciplinary team;
- who require routinely the use of specialist health care equipment or treatments which require the supervision of specialist NHS staff;
- who have a rapidly degenerating or unstable condition which means that they will require specialist medical or nursing supervision.

(DoH 1995a: 15)

As of April 1996, health authorities and local authorities must have in place agreed criteria for assessing eligibility for continuing care financed by the NHS (DoH 1996b).

Terminal care

... as long as we deny the presence of death within the institution, we shall also fail to create an environment that encompasses all aspects of institutional life.

(Peace 1988: 231)

Field and James (1990) show that in 1990 just over half of all deaths in Britain occurred within a hospital environment; 23 per cent in the person's own home; 13 per cent in a nursing or residential home; and 4 per cent in a hospice. Their analysis of the characteristics of death within different settings contrasts the person-centred approaches common to home and hospice with the more organization-centred approaches of homes and hospital where rules, routines and a lack of family involvement are common.

Yet while the hospice model of holistic care remains important, questions are being raised about the future of such provision and its traditional focus on people with cancer (Clark 1990). Given the trend in continuing care outlined above, the number of older people who will die in residential or nursing homes may increase, and yet, to date, little attention has been paid to the circumstances and care of dying persons in homes. Current research by Counsel and Care (1996); Katz *et al.* (1996) aims to shed further light on practice issues surrounding death in homes, and the implications for training and skills development among staff. Within the future debate about the form and function of residential care we will need to look closely at developments in the hospice environment in terms of both bricks and mortar and palliative care skills.

Residential care – one of many options

This discussion of form and function shows us that residential care is increasingly becoming just one of several forms of accommodation and care which may be available. It is a service which provides, in terms of places, the largest share of this type of provision but it is not the fastest-growing sector.

The future form and function of residential care hangs in the balance. On the one hand, those older people who find the emotional and practical resources to plan ahead may opt in greater numbers for supported housing which offers a home for life. Alternatively, those who remain in their own homes may experience an unplanned requirement for nursing home care as an alternative to hospital care at the end of their lives. Residential care homes, in this scenario, face the danger of becoming the providers of a cheaper alternative to nursing home care, where personal care staff continue to straddle the boundaries of personal and nursing care. The evidence considered in this text suggests that this scenario should be resisted by all parties of influence.

6

The market and the state

The wider social and economic context in which care options develop now
merits consideration. Having looked at the role of residential care homes
within our society and the ways in which both the nature of care and the settings in which care is provided have changed, we are now in a position to consider the relationships which exist between the providers and purchasers of
residential care – older people and their families, the care market; and the state.

This consideration must be prefaced by a brief reference to the shifting
political climate within which these relationships have come to be defined.
At the onset of the 1980s, with an incoming radical right government asserting individual and family responsibility for well-being, the fate of vulnerable
elderly people was caught up in a maelstrom of political change. Characterized as the return to Victorian values, government ideology promoted a sharp
move away from direct provision of welfare services by both the central and
the local state towards a system which favoured arrangements for services
that would be under the immediate control of independent care givers, formal
or informal. This philosophy is encapsulated in the 1981 White Paper on old
age:

> Money may be limited but there is no lack of human resources. Nor is
> there any lack of goodwill. An immense contribution is already being
> made to the care and support of elderly people by families, friends and
> neighbours, and by a wide range of private, voluntary and religious
> organisations. We want to encourage those activities so as to develop the
> broadest possible base of services.
>
> (DHSS 1981: 3)

Hence the phrase 'the rolling back of the welfare state' which was used by
social commentators to alert erstwhile welfare beneficiaries and their
advocates to the nature of the impending changes.

Traditionally, older people and their families have been the recipients of particular welfare services as individuals, with accumulated entitlement. They have no history as the major purchaser of residential care. Emerging from the Poor Law traditional response to need, local authorities from 1948 onwards came to be seen as the principal provider of residential care. Until the recent past, the concept of a purchaser (whether that purchaser is a state agency or a fee-paying individual old person) was poorly defined. We are now witnessing some continuities in the pattern of purchase and provision, but equally there are major changes, the consequences of which have yet to be fully understood. Given this complexity and fluidity, we begin this chapter by focusing on the relationship between the state and the care market, returning later to individuals and families, and their place in the scheme of things.

From provider to regulator

The post-war history of residential care up until the 1980s cast the state in the role of major provider. But in the 1980s this role was to change, leading to a fundamental restructuring of the relationships entered into by the state, the market, and individuals and their families with respect to long-term care in later life. It was the rapid (and seemingly uncontrolled) growth of the independent sector during the early 1980s which prompted a public debate about the motivations and characteristics of the new cadre of care entrepreneurs; this, in turn, obliged the state to re-examine its role and responsibility as regulator. The state had inadvertently become a major funder of residential care within the independent sector through the social security system; consequently there was a need to demonstrate public accountability. While families will utilize their own resources directly, and so remain independent of the social security system and the local authority, a degree of protection and security is needed for all users against poor quality or inappropriate provision, particularly in an area where decisions about entering care could be final. One obvious approach to offering a form of protection might be seen in terms of 'consumer' protection, based on the mores of the marketplace. Arguably, with regard to social care services, something more is required; there is a public and moral duty to guard against the risk of exploitation and offer protection against the unseen consequences and uncertainty of the market (Day *et al.* 1996).

Before the expansion of residential home care in the 1980s, a minimalist approach to regulation had been judged adequate for the smaller and fewer concentrations of residential elderly living within homes provided outside of state provision. Clearly, this would not satisfy the wider agenda for the assurance of quality of life that accompanied new forms of care from new providers in a revitalized care market. Confidence levels among the different interested parties needed to be raised. Accordingly, the Registered Homes Act 1984 was enacted. This consolidated earlier legislation around the registration and inspection of private and voluntary residential care, nursing home care and other independent facilities (such as independent acute hospitals) and set out a framework for addressing standards, see Figure 6.1.

Figure 6.1   Legislation forming the basis for regulation of residential care homes and nursing homes

RESIDENTIAL CARE HOMES	NURSING HOMES
Public Health Act 1936	**NURSING HOMES REGISTRATION ACT 1927**
NATIONAL ASSISTANCE ACT 1948	Public Health Act 1936
Mental Health Act 1959	**NURSING HOMES ACT 1963**
RESIDENTIAL HOMES ACT 1980	Mental Health Act 1959 (beginning of regulation of mental nursing homes)
Health & Social Services and Social Security Adjudications Act 1983	**NURSING HOMES ACT 1975**
	Health Service Act 1980
	Health & Social Services and Social Security Adjudications Act 1983 (did not repeal all of legislation concerning nursing homes and mental nursing homes as it did for residential care homes)

REGISTERED HOMES ACT 1984
CHILDREN ACT 1989
NHS & COMMUNITY CARE ACT 1990
Registered Homes (Amendment) Act 1991

Regulations

National Assistance Act (Registration of Homes) Regulations 1949	Nursing Homes and Mental Nursing Homes Regulations 1981
National Assistance Act (Conduct of Homes) Regulations 1962	Amended and Replaced by: NURSING HOMES AND MENTAL NURSING HOMES REGULATIONS 1984
Amended and replaced by: RESIDENTIAL CARE HOMES REGULATIONS 1984	

Codes of Practice

For Residential Care Homes:	For Nursing Homes:
Home Life (CPA, 1984)	*Registration and Inspection of Nursing Homes: A Handbook for Health Authorities* (National Association of Health Authorities 1985)

Registered Homes Tribunals legislation

Child Care Act 1980 (constitution of tribunals to hear appeals in respect of certain voluntary and private children's homes)

Health and Social Services & Social Security Adjudications Act 1983 (Pt III of Schedule 4 introduces tribunal system, builds on childcare model)

REGISTERED HOMES ACT 1984 (Pt III reproduces Pt. III of Schedule 4 of 1983 Act; Act does not extend to Scotland or Northern Ireland)

REGISTERED HOMES TRIBUNAL RULES 1984

The Registered Homes Act represents an advance on its precursors; as with many such legislative frameworks, it has focused on terms of conditions to be met, regulations to be adhered to and ultimately standards to be set. It has thus invited the possibility of a threshold-standards or checklist approach to quality issues. It has focused attention on aspects of home life that are readily amenable to measurement, with minimal attention to the experience of residential living on the part of residents.

Importantly, there was accompanying guidance in the form of the Centre for Policy on Ageing's *Home Life* (CPA 1984) which related to residential care homes; and the handbook *Registration and Inspection of Nursing Homes*, produced by the National Association of Health Authorities and Trusts (1985; 1988), which covered nursing homes. These advisory texts placed great emphasis on good practice, the former more so than the latter. They continue to exert an important influence on care systems. However, they were located – and remain – outside the legal framework. *Home Life* has now been updated as *A Better Home Life* (CPA 1996) to focus upon the care of older people in a range of settings, rather than, as in the 1984 text, upon a range of client groups in the residential setting. There is evidence that good practice, while guided by documents such as these and by other influential reports from the Social Services Inspectorate such as *Homes are for Living In* (DoH 1989b), has been shaped by local interpretation and reconfigured as local guidance (Kellaher *et al.* 1988). This has resulted in variations in the setting of standards across the UK.

The new arrangements required that the costs of setting up registration and inspection units should be met largely through the fee income from regulation. This remains the case to date, though costs have generally exceeded income (Day *et al.* 1996). Given regional diversity in the concentrations of settings to be registered, only some parts of the UK had the (financial and experiential) capacity to support the development of much more sophisticated approaches to the task than others (Kellaher *et al.* 1988). There is evidence to confirm that this variation in the staffing and resourcing for regulatory activity persists (Day *et al.* 1996). At this transitional point in the late 1980s, newly appointed registration and inspection officers came predominantly from the field of social care practice, having previously, for example, headed residential homes, or worked as social workers or establishments managers (Kellaher *et al.* 1988).

The development of the regulatory function

During the mid-1980s, local authority residential sector provision remained outside this legal framework of regulation, but the growth of the independent sector was accompanied by a climate change. On the one hand, independent care providers complained bitterly of an unjust system which required them to finance their own inequitable treatment. They paid to be checked up on, while the local authority homes escaped any such scrutiny. They could see no rationale for applying quality checks to just one part of the system. At the same time, a series of scandals focused media attention on local authority provision (for example Nye Bevan Lodge; see *The Independent*, 22

July 1987: 5). The wide-ranging discussions on the development of community care policy in the late 1980s and the proper place of residential care within a comprehensive and coherent community care system forced this omission to the fore. Consequently, the White Paper, *Caring for People* (DoH 1989a) outlined the 'arm's length inspection units' which would also take on the regulation of public sector provision. It was fully accepted that the broad, local authority umbrella could not guarantee standards in facilities offered by that same local authority.

Accordingly, a cluster of new inspection units has been developed since the enactment of the NHS and Community Care Act in 1990, and these units have taken on a wider remit than earlier registration and inspection teams. Under new powers, the units cover the inspection of all residential and day care services for all sectors and all client groups; they are also responsible for developing regulation for domiciliary services (DoH 1994a; 1994b; Day *et al.* 1996). At the time the Citizen's Charter was launched in 1991 the role of inspection was seen as 'to check that the professional services that the public receive are delivered in the most effective way possible and genuinely meet the needs of those whom they serve' (DoH and Welsh Office 1995: 7).

In 1994, further attempts were made to open up the system to the public by adding to the number of lay members of inspection advisory panels; by introducing lay members to the inspection of residential care homes; and by making inspection reports available for public scrutiny. Greater emphasis was also to be placed on the follow-up to inspection (DoH 1994c). In a recent document on the future of regulation, the Department of Health set out its view of the 'essential principles which any system for the regulation of social services ought to meet':

- protection of the service users by setting, and monitoring compliance with minimum standards;
- even-handed, fair and consistent approach to all providers, i.e. both public and independent sectors;
- reasonable consistency in the standards applied and in the approach to regulation and inspection;
- flexibility to allow regulation to meet the special needs of the different services and client groups;
- consistency so far as possible with the approach to regulation and inspection in other areas of public provision (e.g. schools);
- the reasonable costs of essential regulation should normally be met by those regulated unless there are special reasons suggesting otherwise; if it is decided to subsidise costs for any reason, this should be transparent;
- the system should deliver value for money;
- effective arrangements for monitoring, transparency and accountability;
- effective rights of redress (e.g. appeal) against unfair decisions.

(DoH and Welsh Office 1995: 10)

Within local authorities, the whole issue of quality assurance moved up the

Figure 6.2   A working model of regulation

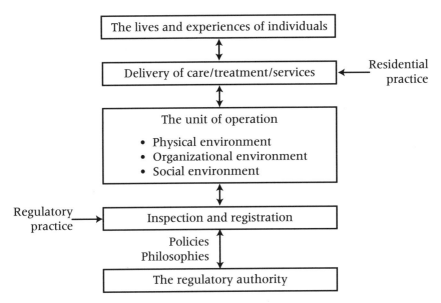

Source: Department of Health and Welsh Office (1990: 44). Crown copyright is reproduced with the permission of the Controller of HMSO.

political and professional agenda throughout the 1980s. Adverse reports on value-for-money studies from the Audit Commission, combined with comment from central government on matters such as choice, customers and the mixed economy of service provision, prompted local authorities to take the business of quality guarantees increasingly seriously. The result has been the establishment of in-house quality agencies, developing sophisticated oversight responsibility for a range of services and with defined systems for handling complaints of poor service.

From bureaucratic to person-centred models of regulation

Much of the research and policy work of the 1970s and 1980s on residential care has centred on ways of developing more individualized approaches within collective settings. To some extent this has been reflected in the way regulatory practice has developed since the enactment of the Registered Homes Act in 1985. Our early work on the development of regulatory practice identified two styles of inspection: the more common one at that time was characterized by an emphasis on the 'paperwork' with resident discussions occupying a less prominent place in inspection. Less frequently observed in our research was an approach which placed the resident viewpoint rather more centrally (Kellaher *et al.* 1988: 72). In the intervening decade, the latter, more resident-centred approach has been increasingly acknowledged as an important aspect of regulatory activity. The shift from a predominantly bureaucratic model of regulation to one that takes account of the people concerned – especially residents – is illustrated in Figure 6.2.

This model of regulation and the place which the lives and experiences of residents should occupy was developed in the course of research which culminated in *Coming to Terms with the Private Sector* (Kellaher *et al.* 1988). It was refined for the Department of Health funded training course for inspection staff, *Making Sense of Inspection* (DoH and Welsh Office 1990) and subsequently formed the basis of thinking for *Inside Quality Assurance* (CESSA 1992). This is a quality assurance pack for use in residential homes, which has the resident at its core. The point to be made here is that while the assessment of fitness of people, building and care plans, through the registration and inspection processes, must have sound administrative underpinnings, essentially it is a process which rests upon the experiences of – and outcome for – residents. Increasingly, the skills necessary for inspection began to focus on ways of gaining a picture of settings as places to live and work, where the balance of interests between staff and residents was crucial and the user was seen as a key source of information.

The shift from bureaucratic to resident emphasis requires an inspectorate that makes complex professional demands of the responsible officer and demands a real mix of skills, experience and response. Such an enhanced role entails the development of skills of observation, interviewing, recording, evaluation and communication. It also rests upon the time resources necessary to build up rapport between regulator and regulated. Yet, the legal requirement is for inspection to be carried out a minimum of twice a year. There is a mass of essential paperwork to be considered, and so, in practice, quantitative tools of inspection (e.g. checklists) have been used more widely than any form of qualitative assessment (Kellaher *et al.* 1988; DoH and Welsh Office 1990; Day *et al.* 1996).

Here we see a tension between a focus on minimum standards and a focus on quality that is predicated on user expectations and experiences rather than those of staff and/or organizations. Both represent aspects of quality in service provision, but they operate at different ends of a spectrum. They also relate to discrete aspects of regulation: the policing of standards and the facilitation and enhancement of good practice. The developmental aspect of inspection is not strictly a statutory duty; yet its role, through, for example, the support for staff training, has been stressed in documents such as *Residential Care: A Positive Choice* (NISW 1988a), *Home Life* (CPA 1984), *A Better Home Life* (CPA 1996) and *Creating a Home from Home: A Guide to Standards* (Residential Forum 1996).

More recent research has shown that for many of the new inspection units, meeting the target of two inspections a year has sometimes proved difficult (DoH 1994a; 1994b; DoH and Welsh Office 1995). Additionally, there is wide variation between inspection units, in terms of personnel, systems, workload and resources. Day *et al.* (1996: 11) comment: 'But whatever the reasons, the variations between inspection units underline the fact that there are 107 different regulatory regimes in England'.

This picture of widespread variation does not inspire confidence that the system of regulation, as it is currently managed and resourced, offers the way

Figure 6.3   Overall climate, individual and organizational interests

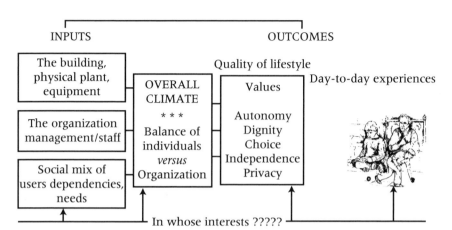

Source: Department of Health and Welsh Office (1990: 67). Crown copyright is reproduced with the permission of the Controller of HMSO.

forward for establishing a universal quality service, albeit that minimum threshold standards can be addressed by this approach. We see evidence that the enforcement, over time, of minimum standards has led to improvement – in, for example, the proportion of single rooms in homes. Thus, it can be argued that the prevailing regulatory system has had some positive benefit, at least for the setting of standards in the traditional 'tape-measure' model of operation (Day *et al.* 1996). The extent to which adjustments in regulatory structure may have led to improvement at the more ephemeral, intangible levels of residential provision may rest upon new understandings of the ways inputs are regulated and matched with residential processes and outcomes. Clearly, regulation is making an impact on assessing inputs, but this may not always ensure the quality of residential experience. Assessment of inputs, if isolated from understandings of day-to-day living and the experiential outcome for those who receive residential services, is unlikely to contribute to the emergence of regulatory structures which are person centred (see Figure 6.3). It may be the case that it is inappropriate to place a person-centred approach within a single regulatory system. It is here that we may need to make the distinction between quality control and quality assurance, following Kellaher and Peace (1993: 168–9):

> Quality control implies quality at a certain level and focuses attention on standards; objective criteria which may be imposed and which outsiders can use to take a snapshot of what is happening. Quality assurance implies that the recipients of a service, and the 'public' at large, should in some way be assured of a certain quality of product which meets their needs. It is a continuous process and consequently, insiders – 'those who really know' – have to be involved.

It is interesting to reflect upon the way in which the quality agenda has shifted over the past half century. Quality is one of those timeless concerns which is increasingly reflected in the policy initiatives of governments, in research and in the literature. The concept is used – and perhaps, on occasion, abused – by different parties, working to different agendas, and with operational definitions of quality that may differ radically in orientation. But it is beyond dispute that residents should, could and do experience quality in their lives and that their perspective is being brought into sharper focus by new emphases on quality assurance.

Developing the practice of quality assurance

Regulatory developments can be traced back to the end of the 1970s and the early 1980s. Professionals acknowledged the need to shift language and practice away from an imperative for quality of care and towards the higher-level concern with quality of life. Quality-of-life ideology encouraged an adjustment on the part of doctors, nurses, social workers and many more, not only to focus attention on the standard of delivery and the unquestioned professionalism of different specialists in the various care services, but also to examine the way in which these same services are experienced by the user. At this time, the designation of 'user' was not yet in vogue, and a transition was in progress in the labelling of older people and others – from patients to clients, to consumers, and later customers (Peace 1993a).

Much of this particular approach to quality, while rarely articulated, was about attributing prestige and a positive image to services that arguably suffered the taint of municipal corporatism. The 1950s and 1960s investments in care were starting to look shabby and lacked any sense of pride. There was an unbroken similarity in design, ethos and way of life in local authority homes, as our earlier text (Willcocks *et al.* 1987) recorded, as well as on geriatric long-stay wards. So, in terms of the individual recipient of services, quality-of-life themes were designed to redirect attention to personal experience and self-defined life satisfaction, in the face of what might be perceived as collectivist threats, leading ultimately to conformity and uniformity. Images persist of passive, sad-faced, elderly residents, poorly groomed and lacking real social stimulus, backs literally to the wall, watching institutional television in the institutional lounge. Contesting the necessity of such arrangements, quality of life came to mean the ability to preserve personal integrity; to exert control in day-to-day activities; to make important decisions; and to be taken seriously.

In terms of the developing quality agenda, the focus on quality-of-life concerns did mean that service specifications – for residential care, home care, nursing care and more – were starting to be interpreted more generously. As a result, considerations of choice, flexibility and customer feedback started to inform the priorities for care providers. Nevertheless, the standards of services were actually laid down by acknowledged professional experts, and a judgement about whether standards had indeed been met was only to be exercised by another set of experts. In other words, quality assessment started to emerge as a real possibility – with public concern being alerted to shortfalls in care provision by a steady flow of high-profile stories through the popular media.

And so, in the mid-1980s, a different battleground was cleared and the struggle for quality control began, influenced by the American managerialist literature on excellence. Here a growing body of professional care managers and care regulators, in health and social services, started to challenge the traditional authority and mystique of the professional care givers. Social Work Services was reborn as the Social Services Inspectorate, and the new cadre of registration/inspection officers, already mentioned, entered the quality business.

In parallel with the development of a regulatory system, we have also seen the emergence of programmes of quality assurance as well as accreditation schemes by independent bodies or associations of providers. Quality assurance programmes operate at the level of the home and focus variously on the quality of management, the mission of the organization, and the relationship between management quality and quality of care provided. O'Kell (1995) recently reported on 11 systems currently in operation. Of these only two – *Homes are for Living In* (DoH 1989b) and *Inside Quality Assurance* (CESSA 1992) – make a deliberate attempt to focus on the relationship between the quality of care provided and the quality of life of residents. Indeed only *Inside Quality Assurance* involves service users directly in evaluating residential life through the construction of a quality group which is charged with listening to those who live and work in the home (Kellaher and Peace 1993; Youll and McCourt-Perring 1994).

The operation of a system of quality assurance within a home is, in itself, seen as an indicator of quality by those responsible for quality control, but there is still a danger that the balance of interests will remain weighted towards the quality of care provided rather than the quality of life experienced. However, the development of quality assurance systems and independent accreditation systems has begun to call into question the continuing need for a state-controlled regulatory system. This process of questioning established regulatory practice gives momentum to the new world of contracting care services.

The relationship between contracting and inspection

The NHS and Community Care Act 1990 introduced what has been called the 'contract culture' into social services. It did this by taking from local authorities the right to be the sole providers of services within their areas, for the people whom they fund, and opening up service provision to competitive tendering from all sectors. But the market which exists in the field of social care clearly does not equate with the wider market for goods and services (Hoyes and Means 1993). In any given area the range of providers and services will vary; they will include the small-scale family business, the national voluntary organization, the big for-profit corporation and many others. And the purchaser will span two extremes, from those individuals and families who can still afford to purchase accommodation and care directly, to the corporate purchaser in the shape of the local social services department – the latter increasingly dominating and determining the future shape of the care business.

Within this scenario, the types of contractual agreement reached between purchaser and providers vary widely. To date a distinction has been made between those social services contracts which are made as a block – where the local authority contracts with a number of providers to provide, for example, a certain number of places in residential care – and those which are individual or spot contracts made on a one-off basis.

Not surprisingly, the degree to which contracts specify the quality of the service to be provided also appears to vary and the variation has been categorized by researchers in different ways. Thus, among a range of types, Flynn and Common (1990) identify those service contracts where greater emphasis is placed on specifying service inputs and contrasts them with those service agreements where greater flexibility is incorporated and the emphasis is shifted towards outputs and outcomes for users. This suggests that the enhancement of provision against required standards within residential care can be made both through contracting and through regulation. It implies that a harmonization between the quality function in contracting and in regulation might be beneficial to different stakeholders. A recent exchange between the providers and purchasers of care, in the form of the British Federation of Care Home Proprietors (BFCHP), and the Association of Directors of Social Services (ADSS) about the 'imposition of' or 'demand for' single-room occupancy in homes, demonstrates a certain tension between two regulatory frameworks: registration/inspection and contracting (ADSS, 1995). The BFCHP–ADSS debate also illustrates an increasing influence, from the market, on the shaping of quality. To date, however, there has been little correspondence between the two systems with regard to long-term care. Indeed, in calling for a review of the regulatory system the Department of Health comments:

> The Government guidance on regulation and inspection under the Registered Homes Act ... reflects the principle that inspection should be carefully focused on the basic statutory standards necessary in order for a service provider to be legally permitted to operate. It recognises that contract standards, set by local authorities as purchasers, may sometimes be higher than those required for registration.
>
> (DoH and Welsh Office 1995: 11)

It is interesting to note that in the area of domiciliary care, where regulation is not mandatory at present, we are beginning to see examples of some integration between the two regulatory forms, where purchasers are liaising with inspectors over approved lists of providers (which may be part of a voluntary accreditation scheme – see London Domiciliary Care Initiative 1993). In such cases, service users may also be involved in the development of service specifications, a practice which has signally failed to develop in relation to long-term care (see, for example, Williams and Dickins 1994).

A call for deregulation

In recent years various factors have led to a call for a review of the regulatory system. There has been an ongoing concern, voiced by providers, that the system places too many burdens on home owners and/or managers. The argument is given that inspectorial systems are time-consuming and laborious in terms of administration. Independent providers have also voiced the view that the development of contractual standards setting, peer pressure to raise standards, the development of quality assurance programmes and accreditation through organizations representing proprietors, for example, render regulation unnecessary (Gladstone 1993). This is coupled with a concern over variations in standards setting and professional practice across the UK and an anxiety that Registered Homes Tribunal cases are taking too long to come to a decision. Accordingly, these structural issues about regulatory practice have been taken on board by a government keen to 'free business from unnecessary burdens and bureaucracy' (DoH and Welsh Office 1995: 8).

Notwithstanding such claims with respect to burdensome procedures, there are frequent evidentially based reminders that parts of the regulatory framework do not function effectively and efficiently. For example, the changing needs of the older population with regard to nursing and personal care place demands on dual-registered facilities which make the dual system of regulation cumbersome and protracted (Gladstone 1993; Eaton 1995; Day et al. 1996).

In responding to these differing types of criticism the Department of Health (DoH and Welsh Office 1995) issued a consultation document, *Moving Forward*, in September 1995, and set up a major review of the regulatory system intended and completed during 1996. Here, a number of questions were to be addressed concerning future arrangements for regulation. Fundamental issues were raised, such as:

- Does the role of statutory regulation need redefining or modifying in the light of the continuing development of other mechanisms for specifying and monitoring standards in social services?
- Should the purpose of the statutory regulation and inspection systems continue to be to define the basic quality standard which a service provider needs to meet in order to be legally permitted to operate?
- Should the standards set for the purpose of statutory regulation continue to be based primarily on the inputs into care?

(DoH and Welsh Office 1995: 11–12)

All the evidence from quality assurance beyond residential services into the broader service domain involving different users or 'customers' (as in education, housing or transport) points to the necessity of engaging with user feedback as an integral part of quality assurance and continuous improvement (Pfeffer and Coote 1991). Quality work cannot be dealt with adequately as a marginal or optional add-on dimension. This suggests that a resolution of issues raised in the consultation document must seek to legitimize the user in any future set of regulatory arrangements.

Other outstanding issues of regulation relate to the even-handedness of those who inspect services across a range of residential care providers; how to improve upon the current system of dual regulation given the local authorities' new role in assessment for nursing home care; the frequency of inspection; the role of inspection within the investigation of complaints by service users; how the cost of regulation should be met; and the question of whether regulation should be run by a body independent of existing statutory bodies. A number of alternative models for a future system were proposed by *Moving Forward*. One option was local regulation with enhanced national input into standards setting; an alternative was the development of a national inspectorate coupled with accreditation through provider organizations. Evidence on effective quality assurance systems confirms that the regulators must have credibility. The challenge is to devise a system where the credibility of professional peers and those with local/regional intelligence can stimulate providers and users alike to participate actively and to positive effect with the new arrangements. At the time of writing the report of the independent assessor, Tom Burgner (1996), has recommended that regulation be kept under local authority control but possibly moved to the trading standards department.

The decisions made about the future of regulation are important not only for the future relationship between the market and the state but also for individuals and their families. Across the political spectrum there is agreement on the need for a body whose role lies to one side of market negotiations. The task is variously defined as monitoring basic standards and facilitating innovations in practice. In the absence of such arrangements, those for whom the unmediated power of organizations will always operate as a barrier will be left unprotected. Dealing with this complex challenge is a prerequisite for all individuals and families and takes precedence over the ability to pay for one's care. While accountability for public moneys is also crucial, protection is of the essence since it underpins the quality of everyday life. This is particularly important in the present climate of uncertainty, where it remains the case that the future of residential care and other forms of long-term support cannot be predicted.

Funding residential care

The future of funding arrangements to support care services for older people is dependent on many interlocking factors:

> Any assessment is greatly complicated by a number of unknown factors which have a major bearing on resource requirements. These include: the extent of self-payment; average lengths of stay in residential and nursing homes; local authorities' revenue from charges for both residential and non-residential services; the strengths of underpinning provided by informal care; and the degree to which home care spending reflects 'diversion' from residential or nursing care or simply additional services for people who would have stayed in their own homes anyway. Moreover, the long term issue is not so much the adequacy of resources now as the willingness of government to respond to inevitable future changes in underlying demand.
>
> (Laing 1995: A198)

In his final sentence, Laing alludes to what he sees as one of the crucial debates of the present time, i.e. the financing of long-term care (Laing 1993). Since the National Assistance Act of 1948, a fundamental divide has existed between the financing of the NHS and the financing of long-term care services. While the former has been dealt with thus far on a universal basis, the latter has been subject to routine (and relatively unchallenged) means-testing. In this sense it remains tied to the legacy of the post-war welfare consensus. Arguably, the health and social care needs of an ageing society at the end of the twentieth century, while often publicly debated, have not been given the attention they deserve. At present almost three-quarters of the long-term care budget is spent on institutional services (NHS or home care settings) as opposed to care for people living within their own homes. Yet, Laing (1993) estimates that while this spending amounts to over £9 billion, the estimated value of unpaid care for older people provided by family and friends is £32.5 billion (both figures at 1992 prices). We cannot avoid posing the question whether the great discrepancy between these two figures obscured the debate which surfaced in May 1996 when Stephen Dorrell, Minister for Health, proposed that the cost of long-term care could now be calculated.

Our prime interest in this book has been with residential care, and we have been able to chart some of the significant changes which have taken place in relation to this provision. However, while there have been changes in the market, and perhaps in the form and the function of residential services, there has been broad-based continuity with respect to the financial arrangements. We saw in Chapter 2 that, at present, more than two-thirds of residents are financed publicly, either totally or in part. Those who own property are currently disregarded from means-tested benefits. Given the rise in home-ownership across the generations, the numbers of those who will pay privately for residential care could be expected to increase. At the same time the government has been at pains to placate those whose assets have denied them means-tested support. Accordingly, they have attempted to modify the system and alter the limit at which assets are disregarded, thus enabling some people either to pay for a more costly style of provision than that purchased through the local authority or to pass on greater assets to other members of the family.

What, then, should happen in the future? Given the future need for a flexible system of long-term care which anticipates and responds to projections of our ageing population, an urgent set of discussions needs to be held among the various interested parties: the state, the providers, families and users (and their representatives). Laing (1993) considers a scenario in which the state takes over responsibility for paying for the long-term care of all older people through a social insurance system. However, he concludes that such a system would exacerbate a range of inequities including those based on property inheritance. As an alternative, he considers that 'the most rational policy option is the partial social insurance model' (Laing 1993: 15), already common in parts of western Europe. In this model a distinction is made between care and hotel costs. Thus long-term care (including nursing and social care) in a residential or nursing home would become a non-means-tested state benefit, subject to an assessment of need, while the hotel element of care would be subject to means-testing (Laing 1993: 16, 125–7). Such a system, he feels, would also stimulate the market for private financial products (such as long-term care insurance). This is an additional form of protection which, to date, has found little take-up. However, in May 1996, the Conservative government published a consultation document on the future funding of long-term care with the intention of introducing legislation in the autumn of 1996, to encourage people to buy insurance policies (DoH 1996b). By stressing that the main responsibility for paying for long-term care should 'rest with the individual', the Health Minister, Stephen Dorrell, outlined a scheme whereby payments from an insurance policy may be offset against any future means test by the state, thus enabling those who can afford to do so to protect a higher proportion of their inheritable assets. This is said to 'reward the thrifty for their responsibility' (*The Guardian*, 8 May 1996), but has been criticized for targeting only those who will be able to afford insurance premiums and for failing to tackle wider concerns over the unpredictability of financial markets.

Furthermore, the fate of those who have either few or no assets or are 'house-rich but income-poor', and who are not happy to borrow against their property, is ignored. Such proposals also appear to be at odds with recent research from the Nuffield Community Care Studies Unit at the University of Leicester which shows that a majority of those interviewed in a national survey thought that the state 'should provide basic services which individuals could supplement if they wished' (ESRC 1996: 8). Thus, policies which sought to finance long-term care costs through the assets of property owners would be at odds with normative views of inheritance.

Radical alternative models are also being explored. At the time of writing, a number of major inquiries into the future funding of long-term or continuing care are reporting. The House of Commons Health Committee have commented that long-term care insurance should be regulated and that private insurance remains too costly for most people (House of Commons Health Committee 1996), whereas the Joseph Rowntree Foundation Inquiry into Meeting the Costs of Continuing Care proposes that care for older people should be free at the point of delivery but supported by a new National Care Insurance scheme, a system of compulsory care insurance contributions introduced in partnership with the private sector (Joseph Rowntree Foundation Inquiry 1996).

Perhaps more fundamental to the way in which residential care develops in the future would be a financial recognition of the work of informal carers plus a devolution of moneys to individuals and carers to spend as they think fit (Laing 1993). At the time of writing, the current debate over the Community Care (Direct Payments) Bill and whether or not to include people over 65 years of age as eligible for direct payments has shifted attention on to resourcing issues (Age Concern 1996). However, the development of a system of brokerage (or vouchers) would need to be paralleled by the development of more widespread, varied and flexible forms of domiciliary, day and respite care. The lack of this range of services in part creates the demand for residential care. While nursing homes and very sheltered housing provide more and more elements of personal care, they have made their market niche around health/tending care and accommodation. Residential care provides companionship, security and care for those who live alone and who are without family members. A key question, however, is whether residential services act as a substitute for care which could be provided at home. And a follow-on question is whether this has become just a question of costs. It is a matter of simple fact that presently we subscribe to a situation where publicly financed residential care is being targeted more and more on a selected group, while those with informal carers go without. The introduction of the Carers (Recognition and Services) Act 1995 and the impact that assessing the needs of care givers alongside care receivers may have on the demand for residential care are as yet uncharted. Scenarios may be envisaged where, on the one hand, the needs of a very stressed care giver override those of the recipient. On the other hand, flexible use of residential care could support home-based care, or informal carers could be encouraged to play an enhanced, but negotiated, role in the residential setting.

In this chapter our concerns have focused on the developing relationships between the state, the market and the family over long-term care for older people. We have charted the tension which exists when government seeks to provide a regulatory system which both protects vulnerable consumers from poor standards of care and frees business from unnecessary bureaucracy. We have also highlighted the ways in which responsibilty for paying for long-term care is shifting from the state evermore towards older people and their families. Consequently, if families are to take on this responsibility and pay for it in ever increasing numbers then for some the power to choose services may become a reality. Throughout this book we have posed a number of far-reaching questions concerning the future of residential care. It now remains for us to try and pull the various strands of our argument together.

7

The new shape of
residential care

Introduction

It is clear that, in the period since 1980, residential care has come to be framed
by at least one set of new influences, those which arise from the NHS and
Community Care Act. The extent to which this legislation is an expression of
society's aspirations for its vulnerable groups, as well as a consequence of the
market influences which preceded its enactment, is a question which runs in
parallel to the questions posed at the start of this book about the changing
shape of residential care. Underpinning this debate are issues of demographic
and economic mass, as these relate to older populations in their community
and family settings.

In order to understand the direction which residential and nursing care
might be taking we need to examine where change has already taken place
and where resistance persists. An analysis of the nature of change – whether
fundamental or cosmetic – and explanations for its introduction and incorpor-
ation will contribute to our understanding of the future of residential care for
older people, as will an analysis of the resistances we have noted. To these
ends we address three critical questions. First, on balance, which way is residential care moving? Second, to what extent has it become a positive choice
for older people? Third, what needs to be set in place to secure a better deal
in residential settings for all concerned?

It is difficult to deny that there is a new mood about residential and nursing
home care. Such a new mood arises, in part at least, from the ideologies which
emerged in the 1980s. The theme of community care, juxtaposed with the
importance of the individual and the need for individuals to pay their own
way in care, represented an 'unpicking' of the post-war consensus. No longer
was it for local authorities to provide settings in which care would be delivered to those assessed as in need of continuous – if not intensive – support.
The homogeneity we observed in our earlier study of a 100 local authority

homes had splintered, as a multitude of small, private sector outlets for care emerged. It is true that a different conformity, one dictated by the economics of care, might be detected, but residential provision does not appear as monolithic as that evident in the late 1970s and early 1980s public sector scene.

The ebbing of a direct local authority influence on the provision of residential care, particularly the case for older people, has also carried the message that there is no longer a municipal 'whipping boy' and that direct responsibility for what happens in residential settings must now rest elsewhere. While the role of the inspectorate has come into sharper focus, the potential for more direct links between those who observe and those who deliver and experience residential care has been enhanced as a consequence of the municipal retreat from the provider role.

The Centre for Policy on Ageing publications *Home Life* (1984) and *A Better Home Life* (1996) – along with *Creating a Home from Home* (1996) as the follow-up to the Wagner reports (NISW 1988a; 1993) – span the decade in which boundaries have been pushed back and residential and nursing home transformation has occurred. Certain entrenchments have, unsurprisingly, also accompanied these changes, but the guidelines and codes of practice show how far aspirations for better residential and nursing home provision emphasize intangible and complex aspects of care.

What has been amenable to change?

In so far as the character of residential and nursing provision has changed, it has done so as a consequence of greater clarity about the people who are involved, notably about residents themselves. It is possible to identify three interrelated aspects of care provision where shifts have occurred.

The first aspect is that of the multiplicity of stakeholders: it is now acknowledged that residential care is constituted through the actions and aspirations of several groups of interested parties, each with a different set of interests. These parties include:

- residents, with their relatives and sometimes their advocates;
- staff, from those responsible for day-to-day delivery of care to those charged with managing care;
- investors, since cross-sectorally care is invested in rather than subsidized;
- regulators, inspectors (professional and lay) and contractors;
- society, both as relative or potential users and as consumers of media opinion.

Second, ideas about the social construction of dependency and about social exclusion for some groups of people have gradually, but perceptibly, come to be acknowledged as credible explanations for many of the difficulties experienced in care by residents and their relatives and friends. Arguments as to whether institutions themselves induce dependency or whether it is a societal structure over which the residential or nursing home can have no influence (Baldwin *et al.* 1993) beg the question as to whether or not these places are a part of society's response to older people; they do not disallow the concepts themselves.

The third aspect concerns empowerment of recipients/clients, and of those delivering care. While it can be said that the idea of empowerment for older people in care settings has now caught on, it remains an idea to be fully enacted. Many of the basic structures are in place; the confidence to influence life in these care settings has, however, yet to establish itself as a habitual response among residents and those around them and on the part of front-line staff.

All these ideas were around in 1987 in embryonic form (Willcocks *et al.* 1987). They are now much more powerfully articulated against the present reality of care issues. For instance, while accounts of scandal and revelations of abuse continue to linger in the air around residential and nursing care, anxiety about such exposés now occurs within the framework the public knows as community care and takes in home care as well as residential care. Associated with – though not necessarily consequent upon – this change in focus, there is in the mid-1990s a reversal of the demand that residential care be eliminated from the care spectrum. There is a new recognition that, for certain groups, the residential home can be an appropriate place to live. Furthermore, properly set up, the residential home might lead to benefit for the community as a whole.

Information about the real character of residential care is still not easy to obtain; those living and working within its boundaries are not always able, or perhaps inclined, to describe or explain their experiences. Uneasiness persists among those not directly involved, about knowing too much of the sequestered character of residential and nursing care. Nevertheless, the boundaries between the community and the residential worlds are more permeable than was the case a decade ago. The introduction of inspection across the sectors, and the increasing sophistication of inspectorial activity – along with the co-ordinating work of the Social Services Inspectorate – have meant that residential care has increasingly come to be regarded as an entity which may become a mainstream form of provision for a minority of people.

The quasi-market nature of residential provision serves to reinforce the greater openness as it contributes to the new mood. As already noted, the concern about elder abuse has, to some extent, shifted from the residential to the domestic locus, with calls for regulatory mechanisms to be devised for home care provision. Concern has increased about the pressures upon carers and the possibility of detrimental consequences for older people and other vulnerable groups.

These changes need to be located and understood within broader demographic shifts, as the economic power exerted by older cohorts increases. This residential expression of demographic and economic factors may be more muted than the communitarian expression, but they have nevertheless led to the emergence of different options in institutional care for older people.

New and emergent options

In response to the legislative, demographic and economic influences noted above, a range of new options is becoming available to potential residents and carers. These can be summarized as follows.

- By sector: the growth of the private care sector has meant a devolution to the level of the residential or nursing home. This might also have entailed a fragmentation in terms of standards, or might be seen as a source of variation for styles and approaches to the provision of care, for people with very different sets of needs, which is to be welcomed.
- By form: nursing and residential care necessarily have a support component; they also have an accommodation or housing component. The form which care provision can now assume may be constructed from more flexible permutation and juxtapositions of these discrete elements which make up residential care than hitherto has been the case.
- By user characteristics: residents and patients are now generally older and frailer, and conditions such as dementia are likely to be present. They may be living alone or supported by networks, but they are now more likely to enter care as one-time owner-occupiers and may have new kinds of assets to convert into care, such as annuities, personal and occupational pensions, and perhaps insurance. Relatives and possibly links with others as advocates may be in evidence.
- By social group: residential options for minority ethnic groups, perhaps in non-traditional form, are now being resourced.
- By contract: to a greater and more explicit degree, the tentative expectations of recipients that they may have some redress, when necessary, arises from their raised profile as purchasers of care.
- By quality: there are new opportunities to say something, for expressing views and ideas about care and what may constitute quality; there are new approaches to the locus of quality and its measurement at both experiential, day-to-day levels and organizationally.

To the extent that residential care has been amenable to change, this is demonstrable in these areas. There are, however, other areas of residential care which have proved more or less resistant to change.

What has been resistant to change?

The appearance of residential care has generally changed, at least in terms of buildings and physical environments. The emergent options just considered suggest that change is not simply cosmetic and may be more than skin deep. But there are serious areas which remain resistant to change. They concern the caring task which is at the heart of residential provision, and attitudes within and beyond residential boundaries.

Despite more explicit nursing and residential categorization, the caring task remains the same, which is to say, it tackles the day-to-day, perhaps petty, dependencies and needs of older people.

- The delivery of residential and nursing care is still very practical and task-centred. Residents continue to wish there was time to talk; staff continue not to have time, the scope, perhaps the skill to talk. Skill mix is not yet a realistic possibility. Dual registration continues, generally, to be a cumbersome device for the integration of social and special nursing support when residents require this mix.

- It is still problematic for residential homes, and also for nursing homes, to face extreme mental, emotional and behavioural demands in residents. Such conditions are seen as deviance. To a lesser extent unusual physical conditions may similarly be regarded with alarm and older people regarded at best as sufferers, at worst as perpetrators to be segregated.
- Care workers for older people still fall generally in manual grades, and the care workforce is vulnerable to competition from local labour markets. Generally, pay is better in local hotels than in residential care. National nursing shortages raise particular difficulties for staff recruitment in nursing homes.
- In terms of the rhetoric of empowerment, not much has actually been given up by management; perhaps secrecy has diminished and more useful information is now available than previously.

The caring task has remained unchanged in that neither training possibilities nor remuneration have, where older people are concerned, significantly improved. These represent structural blockages. There are other, more ambiguous features which may unsettle or impede the establishment of sound structures on which to build future residential edifices.

There are a number of ambiguous features of change/non-change:

- There is a sense of confusion because community care has been flawed in its operation. Very possibly it was flawed conceptually. It was set up to limit and ration residential and other forms of care, but failed to be explicit about this goal; rather it obfuscated, both fiscally and organizationally, and residential provision has suffered as a consequence.
- If the analogy of home, in which residential home stood for domestic home and professional care stood for familial care, has been an obstacle to the emergence of clear directions for residential provision, the idea of flexibility has served to confuse community care, and by extension, residential care.
- The residential myth of domesticity has been transposed to the domiciliary setting with 'domiciliary' standing for 'community'. It is arguable that the same kind of symbolic device which has introduced ambiguity in residential care has been transposed and given new life in the community care setting.

Where explicitness appears to have engendered movement, obfuscation and ambiguity continue to engender stasis in care.

The resolution of the old contradictions about the place of older people in society continues to be an ongoing and unresolved issue which affects the development of residential and nursing provision for this group of people.

- Society continues to be Janus-faced. On the one hand, it does not want to exclude or shelve older people, or to practise an ageist apartheid. On the other hand, society cannot resist the categorization and segregation of older people – in mind, if not in fact. Individuals and society profess care and concern for older people, because they are our future selves. In such a frame it is bad – for individuals and as a society – to exclude older people, to permit their degradation or even their segregation.
- But society may also hate older people because they challenge images of independence and well-being. They put individuals and society in mind of

mortality. Older people may also frequently make very difficult demands which cannot be easily or cheaply met.

- One consequence, writ large in residential and nursing provision, is a degree of support for older people, but it is support predicated on a need to contain or otherwise bound that support and the individuals at which it is directed.
- There appears to be a continued need for a symbol which places older people where society needs them to be; generally this is at its margins. The workhouse can no longer function as a symbol which carries threatening messages. But there is a question as to what now threatens older people and whether new symbolic structures have emerged to carry the message beyond the minority which will experience residential living to the whole.

We can speculate that penury, with the attendant threat of homelessness leading to social isolation, may be the current deconstruction of the workhouse symbol which served for so many decades *pour encourager les autres*, and that residential care now acts as a symbol of these dreads. The proposition is sometimes put forward that a post-war population, free from knowledge and especially from experience of the workhouse, with greater confidence as a consuming cohort, will be immune to the symbolic weight carried in older ideas of residential life. Such optimism may be justified, but we have yet to understand how the residential setting may be a threat to personal integrity and the integrity of the self. We have to concede that, with some few exceptions, residential/nursing provision is still seen as the option of last resort; it is not yet, for most, a *Positive Choice*.

Why have there been these advances and resistances?

It seems clear that, over the last decade, residential care has changed its appearance, and that, in certain respects, standards have been raised. It is rare now, for instance, for three or more older people to share a room; in the early 1980s one in five residents in our national sample shared rooms with at least two others (Peace *et al.* 1982: 32). Such shifts, easily visible in the physical environmental aspects of residential care, do not in themselves change the nature of care. They are, nevertheless, preconditions for change, and may also be indicative of change in other aspects of care which are less easily seen. We can point to reductions in sharing of rooms as a change which appears to have been universally taken on board. The crucial question remains, however, how far the residential option is one for which older people now plan and choose with a lighter heart.

It can be argued that, in some instances, the move to residential care is motivated by a willingness to opt for the supports of residential living. It has also to be said, however, that for a majority of older people continued struggle against admission is the norm; the residential option being the residual option. Of course, this is in line with the prevailing philosophy of community care, that domiciliary rather than residential support should be preferable on all counts. But there appear to be other influences which continue to set residential care apart as an option.

One of these is the enormous effort which residents still have to make in order to support and maintain a sense of self in the institutional setting. In our earlier study we noted that residents engaged in actions which could be interpreted as defensive of the self and of territory to buttress the self, within the collectivity and against the very strong organizational current which typically prevail. Much of the behaviour of older people in residential settings continues to be guarded. That is to say, connections between residents are still tentative and characterized by careful distancing. While physical environments, as already noted, have changed considerably, and residential settings are often extremely welcoming, there continues to be resistance and reluctance to engage. How is this wariness to be explained beyond the guardedness which might reasonably be expected of people unconnected by kinship or by locality or history?

It can also be argued that the majority of older people, when they come to consider the options for coping as they become frailer in old age, continue to put aside, if not reject, the residential option. Such sidelining is not because it is a glaringly cruel, institutional, phenomenon; it clearly is not. We would argue that because residential care is still perceived as a serious threat to the self, potential residents are compelled to resist, even when the need for the benefits and supports on offer is overwhelming. Losing individuality, even when losing control is accepted, is not to be countenanced. Very recently published research suggests that depression has an important part to play in the way older people relate to their residential setting (Schneider *et al.* 1996). These recent findings echo the earlier work on relocation (Tobin and Lieberman 1976) in linking threats to personal integrity with the move to residential care.

Peace *et al.* (1982) put forward a model of the residential process. The elements in this model included: physical environment, institutional regime, the mix of residents in a home and the individual older person – or consumer of care. The model identified the influences between these elements and a number of missing links, notably:

> The physical environment can have a direct effect on the life-style of the individual – the lack of single rooms may limit the development of individual pursuits and oblige residents to live a public life . . . it is unusual for the resident to influence the physical environment directly . . . it is rare for the individual resident to make an impact on the institutional environment.
>
> (Peace *et al.* 1982: 49)

There are now settings in which these links, between individual influence and institutional and physical aspects of provision are stronger. Observations in the course of recent work (Kellaher forthcoming), particularly in some voluntary residential settings suggest that residents – even quite frail residents – register a sense of control over the place in which they live and of influence in interaction with those who care for and support them. These settings are, however, still in a minority and the fact that voluntary sector agencies feature here may be attributable to the possibility that *communitaire* philosophies predispose these organizations to structuring the defense of self for both residents and staff. The fact, however, that residents more frequently still express the view 'I didn't think it would come to this' suggests that the experience of control and influence remains a minority experience and that older people fear the dissolution of self which, it is arguable, residential living continues to entail.

This discussion about the defence of self and of personal integrity might be read as relevant only to the – possibly declining – population of residents who remain cognitively intact. But this is not so; it is equally relevant, perhaps more so, to residents whose cognitive capacities are seriously impaired. The dementia mapping work for which Kitwood makes the case (Kitwood 1992; Kitwood and Bredin 1992) is based upon the requirement that someone be in touch with the self which has become impaired. The resident may not be able to demonstrate such a connection: the care worker must act as advocate and substitute. The point to be made here is that it is the connection with self which is central. The staff act as conduits of self.

If it is true that residents and potential residents continue to exhibit determination to avoid what increasingly appear to be settings which are warm, comfortable and reliable places, and safer and more convenient than many of the domestic settings in which older people live, we have to ask what it is that older people see as threatening in settings where the explicit goal is to care. Our response is that the threat to the self is so serious that older people only capitulate after considerable erosion of will has occurred, and they invariably live to regret the lapse in their defences. It is not the move from home which is necessarily threatening; older people move to sheltered housing – admittedly sometimes with regret – but not with the extreme trepidation which frequently accompanies a move to residential care.

It is heartening that some of the new forms of care provision do not appear to strike the same kind of fear, but these are still in the minority. Until residential care clearly and routinely takes account of and supports the self, it will remain a feared – and therefore residual rather than chosen – option. There are signs that this is possible, even though still rare; it is not a structurally impossible eventuality.

Getting real about residential and nursing homes

The point has already been made that a number of realities about residential care need to be recognized and made explicit. The multiplicity of interests have been cited; they must be valued individually for themselves rather than being seen as homogenous residential ingredients with undifferentiated levels of power. There is a need to establish an explicit balance so that no one group's interests are denied, subverted or suppressed.

There must be recognition that there is no monolithic solution, there must be flexible options and flexible frameworks for support and regulation of residential care which extend well beyond the crude mechanism we know as dual registration.

Powerful social and cultural conduits or carriers are required which will allow a better balancing act to take place between the different sets of interests. These conduits might be:

- acknowledging and paying for a skills mix which integrates practical and emotional care;
- installation of appropriate quality systems which allow comment from all sets of interests to become structurally legitimate;
- a framework for local accountability and responsibility which takes on board informal and formal regulatory influences;
- the recognition that design and practice recommendations will only work where there are accurate understandings about the residential implications of proper resourcing of infrastructures.

The place of older people in the wider society must be fairly considered. The possibility that there might be good institutions within a society where attitudes to older people are less than good brings us to the notion of asylum. But the better approach must be a society which contracts with its older people in a much more honest way. It cannot promise miracles, rather, it agrees to undertake residential provision openly and properly.

The opening up of care to market forces has been beneficial in that the potential for new thinking has been unlocked. But it has also had detrimental consequences in that block treatment continues because economies of scale are seen to be essential where care is either continuous and/or demanding of special skills. Serious and obvious obstacles remain in terms of the design of buildings and the poor pay and paucity of training of staff. The invisible obstacles may be more problematic. Yet residential care, in this new-deal sense, will always be necessary for a minority of older people and their families.

Conclusion

Fifteen years ago, writing about residential provision which was predominantly public sector determined, we argued that the physical environment be shaped so that emphasis should shift from the public reality of residential living to the more private possibilities of a life in care, protected from the overwhelming organizational influences. We proposed the residential flatlet as an environmental strategy which could support older people who had become frail in certain ways. We had in view the physical frailties which may accompany advancing years and also the individualities which may have been bruised in the move from home to care, at ages when other 'assaults' on self-esteem may have been sustained. The residential flatlet was to be a base for re-establishing individuality. The evidence – in new building as well as older – suggests that the features physically expressed in the residential flatlet have been taken on board. Residential environments now permit more privacy and individuality, with the potential for support and conviviality. And yet older people are still wary.

We have argued here that this wariness is justified in so far as residential settings still represent a threat not to individuality but, much more profoundly, to the sense of self. The challenge is to construct residential environments which respect older people's pressing urge – however much in need of support and surveillance they may be – to maintain a sense of self. The organizational equivalent of the residential flatlet must be conceptualized and the territory to support the self be carved out of the residential organization. The challenge is to reposition the features which represent the essence of the residential flatlet so that the non-material world of care serves to support older people at the level of the self; the sometimes worn and damaged mind to be supported in the sometimes worn body.

Bibliography

Age Concern (1995a) *NHS Responsibilities for Continuing Health Care and Hospital Discharge Arrangements*, Age Concern Briefings, March. London: Age Concern.

Age Concern (1995b) *Inquiry into Long-term Care – Evidence to the Health Select Committee by Age Concern (the National Council on Ageing)*. London: Age Concern.

Age Concern (1996) Tory rebel brings over-65s into community care cash scheme. *Reportage, Age Concern's Parliamentary Bulletin*, 2(5): 3.

Agich, G.J. (1993) *Autonomy and Long Term Care*. Oxford: Oxford University Press.

Allen, I., Hogg, D. and Peace, S. (1992) *Elderly People: Choice, Participation and Satisfaction*. London: Policy Studies Institute.

Arber, S. and Ginn, J. (1990) The meaning of informal care: gender and the contributions of elderly people. *Ageing and Society*, 10(4): 429–54.

Arber, S. and Ginn, J. (1991) *Gender and Later Life: A Sociological Analysis of Resources and Constraints*. London: Sage Publications.

Arnold, P., Bochel, H., Broadhurst, S. and Page, D. (1993) *Community Care: The Housing Dimension*. York: Joseph Rowntree Foundation.

Association of Community Health Councils for England and Wales (1990) *NHS Continuing Care of Elderly People*. London: ACHCEW.

Association of Directors of Social Services (1995) *A Room of One's Own*. Northallerton: ADSS.

Audit Commission (1985) *Managing Social Services for the Elderly More Effectively*. London: HMSO.

Audit Commission (1986) *Making a Reality of Community Care*. London: HMSO.

Baldwin, N., Harris, J. and Kelly, D. (1993) Institutionalisation: why blame the institution? *Ageing and Society*, 13(1): 69–81.

Balloch, S., Andrew, T., Ginn, J., McLean, J., Pahl, J. and Williams, J. (1995) *Working in the Social Services*. London: NISW.

Barton, R. (1959) *Institutional Neurosis*. Bristol: John Wright.

Bendle, S. (1994) The housing association perspective. In E. Murphy, J. Lindesay and R. Dean, *The Domus Project: Long-Term Care for People with Dementia*. London: The Sainsbury Centre for Mental Health.

Bennett, C. (1994) 'Ending up', *The Guardian Weekend*, 8 October: 12–20.

Beveridge, Sir William (1942) *Social Insurance and Allied Services*, Cmd 6404. London: HMSO.

Biggs, S., Phillipson, C. and Kingston, P. (1995) *Elder Abuse in Perspective*. Buckingham: Open University Press.

Blakemore, K. and Boneham, M. (1994) *Age, Race and Ethnicity*. Buckingham: Open University Press.

Bond, J. (1993) Living arrangements of elderly people. In J. Bond, P. Coleman and S. Peace (eds), *Ageing in Society*. London: Sage Publications, 200–225.

Bond, S. and Bond, J. (1989) *Evaluation of Continuing-care Accommodation for Elderly People. A Multiple-case study of NHS Hospital Wards and Nursing Homes: Some Aspects of Structure and Outcome*. Report No.38(3), Health Care Research Unit, University of Newcastle upon Tyne.

Booth, C. (1889) *Life and Labour of the People in London*. London: Macmillan.

Booth, T. (1985) *Home Truths: Old People's Homes and the Outcome of Care*. Aldershot: Gower.

Booth, T. (1993) Obstacles to the development of user-centred services. In J. Johnson and R. Slater (eds), *Ageing and Later Life*. London: Sage Publications.

Bornat, J., Dimmock, B., Jones, D. and Peace, S. (forthcoming) *Older People and Family Change*. Research Report, School of Health and Social Welfare, Open University: Milton Keynes.

Brearley, P. (1990) *Working in Residential Homes for Elderly People*. London: Routledge.

Brown, H. and Smith, H. (1989) Whose 'ordinary life' is it anyway? *Disability, Handicap and Society*, 4(2) :105–19.

Brown, H. and Smith,H. (eds) (1992) *Normalization: A Reader for the 90s*. London: Routledge.

Bulmer, M. (1987) *The Social Basis of Community Care*. London: Allen and Unwin.

Burgner, T. (1996) *The Regulation and Inspection of Social Services*. London: HMSO.

Bytheway, B. (1982) Review symposium. *Ageing and Society*, 2(3): 389–91.

Bytheway, B. (1995) *Ageism*. Buckingham: Open University Press.

Bytheway, B. and Johnson, J. (1990) On defining ageism. *Critical Social Policy*, 27: 27–39.

Caldock, K. (1994) *Not a Positive Choice: Elderly People Under Pressure to Enter Residential Care*. Research Paper, Centre for Social Policy Research and Development, University of Wales: Bangor.

Cassam, S. and George, C. (1992) *Standard Setting in Nursing Homes and Social Care Homes*: The Pre-cursor to Quality Assurance. Whitley Delamere, Cheshire: Whitley Delamere Consulting Group.

Centre for Environmental and Social Studies in Ageing (CESSA) (1992) *Inside Quality Assurance*. London: CESSA, University of North London.

Centre for Policy on Ageing (1984) *Home Life: A Code of Practice for Residential Care*, Report of a Working Party sponsored by the Department of Health and Social Security and convened by the Centre for Policy on Ageing under the Chairmanship of Kina, Lady Avebury. London: Centre for Policy on Ageing.

Centre for Policy on Ageing (1996) *A Better Home Life*. London: Centre for Policy on Ageing.

Challis, L. and Bartlett, H. (1988) *Old and Ill: Private Nursing Homes for Elderly People*, Age Concern Institute of Gerontology Research Paper No.1. Mitcham, Surrey: Age Concern England.

Chappell, A.L. (1992) Towards a sociological critique of the normalisation principle. *Disability, Handicap and Society*, 7(1): 35–52.

Charlesworth, A., Wilkin, D. and Durie, A. (1984) *Carers and Services: A Comparison of Men and Women Caring for Dependent Elderly People*. Manchester: Equal Opportunities Commission.

Clark, D. (1990) Whither the hospices? In D. Clark (ed.), *The Future for Palliative Care: Issues of Policy and Practice*. Buckingham: Open University Press, 167–77.

Clarke, P. and Bowling, A. (1990) Quality of everyday life in long-stay institutions for the elderly. An observational study of long-stay hospital and nursing home care. *Social Science and Medicine*, 30(11): 1201–10.

Coates, R. and Silburn, D. (1970) *Poverty: The Forgotten Englishman.*

Collopy, B.J. (1988) Autonomy in long term care: some crucial distinctions. *The Gerontologist*, 28 (Supplement), June: 10–17.

Cooper, R., Watson, L. and Allan, G. (1994) *Shared Living: Social Relations in Supported Housing*, Social Services Monographs: Research in Practice. University of Sheffield: Joint Unit for Social Services Research and Community Care.

Counsel and Care (1991) *Not Such Private Places: A Study of Privacy and the Lack of Privacy for Residents in Private and Voluntary Residential and Nursing Homes in Greater London.* London: Counsel and Care.

Counsel and Care (1992a) *From Home to a Home: A Study of Older People's Hopes, Expectations and Experiences of Residential Care.* London: Counsel and Care.

Counsel and Care (1992b) *What If They Hurt Themselves? A Discussion Document on the Uses and Abuses of Restraint in Residential and Nursing Homes for Older People.* London: Counsel and Care.

Dalley, G. (1988) *Ideologies of Caring: Rethinking Community and Collectivism.* Basingstoke: Macmillan Educational.

Dalley, G. (1993) Caring: a legitimate interest of older women. In M. Bernard and K. Meade (eds), *Women Come of Age.* London: Edward Arnold.

Davies, B. and Knapp, M. (1981) *Old People's Homes and the Production of Welfare.* London: Routledge and Kegan Paul.

Day, P., Klein, R. and Redmayne, S. (1996) *Why Regulate? Regulating Residential Care for Elderly People.* Bristol: The Policy Press in association with the Joseph Rowntree Foundation.

Department of Health (1989a) *Caring for People: Community Care in the Next Decade and Beyond.* Cmnd. 849. London: HMSO.

Department of Health (1989b) *Homes are for Living In: A Model for Evaluating Quality of Care Provided, and Quality of Life Experienced, in Residential Care Homes for Elderly People.* Social Services Inspectorate. London: HMSO.

Department of Health (1991) *Registered Homes (Amendment) Act 1991.* London: HMSO.

Department of Health (1992) *The Health of the Nation: A Strategy for Health in England*, Cm. 9186. London: HMSO.

Department of Health (1992) *The Health of Elderly People: An Epidemiological Overview. Vol. 1. Companion Papers*, Central Health Monitoring Unit, Epidemiological Overview Series. London: HMSO.

Department of Health (1993) *Inspecting for Quality: Standards for the Residential Care of Elderly People with Mental Disorders*, Social Services Inspectorate. London: HMSO.

Department of Health (1994a) *Social Services Department Inspection Units: The First Eighteen Months. Report of an Inspection of the Work of Inspection Units in Ten Local Authorities*, Social Services Inspectorate. DoH. London: HMSO.

Department of Health (1994b) *Social Services Department Inspection Units: Report of an Inspection of the Work of Inspection Units in Twenty Seven Local Authorities*, Social Services Inspectorate, Inspection Division. London: HMSO.

Department of Health (1994c) *Inspecting Social Services*, Circular LAC(94)16. London: HMSO.

Department of Health (1995a) *NHS Responsibilities for Meeting Continuing Health Care Needs*, HSG(95)8, LAC (95)5. London: HMSO.

Department of Health (1995b) *Residential Accommodation for Elderly People and People with Physical and/or Sensory Disabilities, Local Authority Supported Residents, Year Ending 31 March 1994, England.* London: Government Statistical Service.

Department of Health (1995c) *Residential Accommodation for Elderly People and People with Physical and/or Sensory Disabilities. All Residents in Local Authority, Voluntary and Private Homes, Year Ending 31 March 1989 to Year Ending 31 March 1994, England,* RA/94/2. London: Government Statistical Service.

Department of Health (1995d) *Residential Accommodation Statistics, 1995,* Statistical Bulletin. London: Government Statistical Service.

Department of Health (1995e) *Report of the Social Services Inspection Units – Third Overview: Report of an Inspection of the Work of Inspection Units on Nineteen Local Authorities,* Social Services Inspectorate London: HMSO.

Department of Health (1996a) *A New Partnership for Care in Old Age: A Consultation Paper,* Chancellor of the Exchequer and Secretary of State for Social Security. London: HMSO.

Department of Health (1996b) *NHS Responsibilities for Meeting Continuing Health Needs – Current Progress and Future Priorities.* London: HMSO.

Department of Health and Welsh Office (1990) *Making Sense of Inspection: A Training Course for Registration and Inspection Staff.* London: HMSO.

Department of Health and Welsh Office (1995) *Moving Forward: A Consultation Document on the Regulation and Inspection of Social Services.* London: HMSO.

Department of Health and Social Security (1971) *Annual Report 1970,* Cmnd. 4714. London: HMSO.

Department of Health and Social Security (1972a) *Annual Report of the Department of Health and Social Security for the year 1971.* Cmnd. 5019. London: HMSO.

Department of Health and Social Security (1972b) *Memorandum – Services for Mental Illness Related to Old Age,* HM(72)71. London: HMSO.

Department of Health and Social Security (1973) *Annual Report 1972.* Cmnd. 5352. London: HMSO.

Department of Health and Social Security (1975) *Annual Report 1974.* Cmnd. 6150. London: HMSO.

Department of Health and Social Security (1977) *Annual Report 1976.* Cmnd. 6931. London: HMSO.

Department of Health and Social Security (1981) *Growing Older,* Cmnd. 8173. London: HMSO.

Department of Health and Social Security (1987) *Public Support for Residential Care. Report of a Joint Central and Local Government Working Party.* (Firth Report). London: HMSO.

Department of Health and Social Security and Welsh Office (1973) *Local Authority Building Note No. 2: Residential Accommodation for Elderly People.* London: HMSO.

Department of Health and Social Security and Welsh Office (1978) *A Happier Old Age: A Discussion Document on Elderly People in Our Society.* London: HMSO.

Department of Health and Social Security and Welsh Office (1982) *A Good Home. A Consultative Document on the Registration System for Accommodation Registered under the Residential Homes Act 1980.* London: HMSO.

Department of Trade and Industry (1987) BS5750/ISO900. *A Positive Contribution to Better Business.* Milton Keynes: BSI–Quality Assurance.

Department of Trade and Industry (1991) *A Positive Contribution to Better Business Issued as a Contribution of the DTI's Effort to Promote Total Quality Management.* London: DTI.

Dixon, S. (1991) *Autonomy and Dependency in Residential Care.* London: Age Concern Institute of Gerontology.

Dunlop, A. (1994) *Hard Architecture and Human Scale: Designing for Disorientation.* Dementia Services Development Centre, University of Stirling.

Eaton, L. (1995) Dual care. *Community Care,* 3 February: 24.

Economic and Social Research Council (1996) Paying for care in old age. *Choice and Beliefs,* newsletter of the ESRC Research Programme on Economic Beliefs and Behaviour, issue 2, May 1996.

Elkan, R. and Kelly, D. (1991) *A Window in Homes: Links between Residential Care Homes and the Community.* London: Social Care Association.

Erikson, E.H. (1982) *The Life Cycle Completed: A Review.* New York: Norton.

Evans, G., Hughes, B. and Wilkin, D. with Jolley, D. (1981) *The Management of Mental and Physical Impairment in Non-specialist Residential Homes for the Elderly,* Research Report No. 4. Department of Psychiatry and Community Medicine, University of Manchester.

Field, D. and James, N. (1990) Where and how people die. In D. Clark (ed.), *The Future of Palliative Care: Issues of Policy and Practice.* Buckingham: Open University Press, 6–29.

Finch, J. (1984) Community care: developing non-sexist alternatives. *Critical Social Policy,* 3(9): 6–18.

Finch, J. (1989) *Family Obligations and Social Change.* Cambridge: Polity Press.

Finch, J. (1995) Responsibilities, obligations and commitments. In I. Allen and E. Perkins (eds), *The Future of Family Care,* London: HMSO, 51–64.

Finch, J. and Groves, D. (1980) Community care and the family: a case for equal opportunities. *Journal of Social Policy,* 9(4): 487–511.

Finch, J. and Groves, D. (1982) By women for women: caring for the frail elderly. *Women's Studies International Forum,* 5(5): 427–38.

Finch, J. and Groves, D. (eds) (1983) *A Labour of Love: Women, Work and Caring.* London: Routledge and Kegan Paul.

Finch, J. and Mason, J. (1992) *Negotiating Family Responsibilities.* London: Routledge.

Flynn, N. and Common, R. (1990) *Contracts for Community Care.* DoH Implementation Document. London: HMSO.

Forrest, R., Murie, A. and Williams, P. (1990) *Home Ownership.* London: Unwin Hyman.

Foucault, M. (1967) *Madness and Civilization.* London: Routledge.

Foucault, M. (1977) *Discipline and Punish: The Birth of the Prison,* trans. Alan Sherridan. London: Allen Lane.

Gavilan, H. (1990) Care in the community: issues of dependency and control – the similarities between institution and home. *Generations Review,* 2(4): 9–11.

Gibbs, I. and Sinclair, I. (1992) Residential care for elderly people: the correlates of quality. *Ageing and Society,* 12(4): 463–82.

Gladstone, D. (1993) *The Deregulation of Nursing and Residential Homes: An Initial Discussion Document.* London: Independent Healthcare Association.

Godlove, C., Richard, L. and Rodwell, G. (1982) *Time for Action: An Observational Study of Elderly People in Four Different Care Environments,* Social Services Monographs, Research in Practice. Joint Unit for Social Services Research and Community Care, University of Sheffield.

Goffman, E. (1961) *Asylums.* London: Penguin.

Goffman, E. (1968) *Stigma.* London: Penguin.

Graham, H. (1983) Care: a labour of love. In J. Finch and D. Groves (eds), *A Labour of Love: Women, Work and Caring,* London: Routledge and Kegan Paul.

Green, H. (1988) *Informal Carers,* OPCS Series GHS No. 15. Supplement A. London: HMSO.

Greenwell, S. (1989) *Whose Life Is It Anyway?: An Action Research Project Surrounding the Development of a Residential and Day-care Facility for Older People.* School of Social Sciences, University of Bath.

Griffiths, R. (1988) *Community Care: An Agenda for Action.* London: HMSO.

Groves, D. (1995) Costing a fortune? Pensioners' financial resources in the context of community care. In A. Allen and E. Perkins (eds), *The Future of Family Care for Older People.* London: HMSO.

Grundy, E. (1992a) Socio-demographic variation in rates of movement into institutions among elderly people in England and Wales: an analysis of linked census and mortality data 1971–1985. *Population Studies,* 46: 65–84.

Grundy, E. (1992b) Socio-demographic change. In Department of Health, *The Health of Elderly People: An Epidemiological Overview. Vol. 1. Companion Papers.* London: HMSO.

Gubrium, J.F. (1975) *Living and Dying in Murray Manor*. New York: St Martin's.

Gubrium, J.F. (1993) *Speaking of Life: Horizons of Meaning for Nursing Home Residents*. New York: Aldine de Gruyter.

Hamnett, C. (1995) Housing equity release and inheritance. In I. Allen and E. Perkins (eds), *The Future of Family Care for Older People*. London: HMSO, 163–80.

Hamnett, C. and Mullings, B. (1992) The distribution of public and private residential homes for elderly persons in England and Wales. *Area*, 24(2): 130–44.

Hamnett, C., Harmer, M. and Williams, P. (1991) *Safe as Houses: Housing Inheritance in Britain*. London: Paul Chapman.

Hanson, J. (1972) *Residential Care Observed*. London: Age Concern England and National Institute of Social Work.

Hazan, H. (1980) *The Limbo People: The Study of the Constitution of the Time Universe among the Aged*. London: Routledge and Kegan Paul.

Hazan, H. (1992) *Managing Change in Old Age: The Control of Meaning in an Institutional Setting*. Albany: State University of New York Press.

Health Advisory Service (1982) *The Rising Tide: Developing Services for Mental Illness in Old Age*. London: Health Advisory Service.

Hepworth, M. (1995) Social gerontology and the sociology of deviance. Paper presented at the Brisitish Society of Gerontology Annual Conference, University of Keele, September.

Hiatt, L. (1980) Disorientation is more than a state of mind. *Nursing Home*, July/August: 30–6.

Higgs, P. and Victor, C. (1993) Institutional care and the life course. In S. Arber and M. Evandrou (eds), *Ageing, Independence and the Life Course*. London: Jessica Kingsley: 186–200.

Hockey, J. (1989) Residential care and the maintenance of social identity: negotiating the transition to institutional life. In M. Jefferys (ed.), *Growing Old in the Twentieth Century*. London: Routledge.

Hockey, J. and James, A. (1993) *Growing Up and Growing Old: Ageing and Dependency in the Life Course*. London: Sage Publications.

Hofland, B.F. (1988) Autonomy in long term care: background issues and a programmactic response. *The Gerontologist*, 28 (Supplement), June: 3–9.

House of Commons Health Committee (1996) *Long-term Care: Future Provision and Funding*, House of Commons Health Committee third report, Session 1995–96. Volume I, HC 59-I. London: HMSO.

Hoyes, L. and Means, R. (1993) Markets, contracts and social care services: prospects and problems. In J. Bornat, C. Pereira, D. Pilgrim and F. Williams (eds), *Community Care: A Reader*. London: Macmillan, 276–86.

Hoyes, L., Lart, R., Means, R. and Taylor, M. (1994) *Community Care in Transition*. York: Joseph Rowntree Foundation.

Hughes, B. and Wilkin, D. (1987) Physical care and the quality of life in residential homes. *Ageing and Society*, 7(4): 399–426.

Hunter, D. (1992) The prospects for long-term care: current policy and realistic alternatives. In L. Gormally (ed.), *The Dependent Elderly: Autonomy, Justice and Quality of Care*. Cambridge: Cambridge University Press.

Ignatieff, M. (1983) Total institutions and working classes: a review essay. *History Workshop Journal*, 15 (Spring): 167–73.

Johnson, J. and Bytheway, B. (1993) Ageism: concept and definition. In J. Johnson and R. Slater (eds), *Ageing and Later Life*. London: Sage Publications.

Johnson, P. (1992) *Income: Pensions, earnings and savings in the Third Age*. Carnegie Inquiry into the Third Age, Research Paper. No. 2. Dunfermline: Carnegie UK Trust.

Jones, A. (1994) *The Numbers Game: Black and Minority Ethnic Elders and Sheltered Housing*. Oxford: Anchor Housing Trust.

Jones, K. and Fowles, A.J. (1984) *Ideas on Institutions: Analysing the Literature on Long Term Care and Custody*. London: Routledge and Kegan Paul.

Joseph Rowntree Foundation (1994) NVQs in residential homes. In *Social Care Briefings*, September. York: Joseph Rowntree Foundation.

Joseph Rowntree Foundation Inquiry (1996) *Meeting the Costs of Continuing Care: Recommendations*. York: Joseph Rowntree Foundation.

Judge, K. and Sinclair, I. (eds) (1986) *Residential Care for Elderly People*. London: HMSO.

Katz, J., Komaromy, C. and Sidell, M. (1996) *Death and Dying in Residential Settings for Older People. Stage One Findings*. School of Health and Social Welfare. The Open University, Milton Keynes.

Kayser-Jones, J.S. (1981) *Old, Alone and Neglected: Care of the Aged in Scotland and the United States*. Berkeley: University of California Press.

Kellaher, L. (forthcoming) *Quality Matters*. St Albans: The Abbeyfield Society.

Kellaher, L. and Peace, S. (1990) Triangulating data. In S. Peace (ed.), *Researching Social Gerontology*. London: Sage Publications.

Kellaher, L. and Peace, S. (1993) Rest assured: new moves in quality assurance for residential care. In J. Johnson and R. Slater (eds), *Ageing and Later Life*. London: Sage Publications, 168–77.

Kellaher, L., Peace, S., Weaver, T. and Willcocks, D. (1988) *Coming to Terms with the Private Sector: Public Sector Responses to New Legislation*. London: PNL Press.

Kellaher, L., Peace, S. and Willcocks, D. (1985) *Living in Homes: A Consumer View of Old People's Homes*. London: Centre for Environmental and Social Studies in Ageing, Polytechnic of North London and British Association of Service to the Elderly.

Kelman, H. (1973) Violence without moral restraint. *Journal of Social Issues*, 29: 30–41.

Kent County Council (1991) *Good Care: A Guide to the Good Care of Older People in Residential Homes*. Maidstone: Kent County Council.

Kitwood, T. (1992) Towards a theory of dementia care: personhood and wellbeing. *Ageing and Society*, 12: 269–87.

Kitwood, T. and Bredin, K. (1992) *Evaluating Dementia Care: The DCM Method*. Bradford Demential Research Group, University of Bradford.

Kitwood, T., Beckland, S. and Petre, T. (1995) *Brighter Futures*. Oxford: Anchor Housing Association.

Knapp, M. (1981) *The Economics of Social Care*. London: Macmillan.

Laing, W. (1993) *Financing Long-term Care: The Crucial Debate*. London: Age Concern England Books.

Laing, W. (1995) *Laing's Review of Private Healthcare, 1995*. London: Laing and Buisson Publications.

Lansbury, G. (1928) *My Life*. London: Constable and Co.

Larder, D., Day, P. and Klein, R. (1986) *Institutional Care for the Elderly: the Geographical Distribution of the Public/Private Mix in England*, Bath Social Papers. No. 10, University of Bath.

Lawrence, S., Walker, A. and Willcocks, D. (1987) *She's Leaving Home*. London: PNL Press.

Lawton, M.P. (1980) *Environment and Aging*. Monterey, California: Brooks/Cole.

Layder, D. (1994) *Understanding Social Theory*. London: Sage Publications.

Lee-Treweek, G.A. (1994) Discourse, care and control: an ethnography of residential and nursing home elder care work. Unpublished PhD thesis, University of Plymouth.

Lee-Treweek, G.A. (1995) *Understanding Paid Care Work – Towards a New Critique*. Occasional Papers in Sociology Series, University of Manchester, Spring.

Levin, E., Sinclair, I.A.C. and Gorbach, P. (1989) *Families, Services and Confusion in Old Age*. Aldershot: Gower.

Lewis, J. and Meredith, B. (1988) *Daughters who Care*. London: Routledge.

Lloyd, P. and Austin Locke, J. (1995) Sheltered housing and the care of the increasingly frail. Paper presented at the Annual Conference of the British Society of Gerontology, University of Keele, September.

Local Government Information Unit (1993) *Caught in the Care Trap: Income Support for Private and Voluntary Residential and Nursing Home Fees,* London: LGIU.

London Domiciliary Care Initiative (1993) *The London Domiciliary Care Initiative.* London: LDCI.

Marchant, C. (1995) Hard times. *Community Care,* 26 January: 16–19.

Mackintosh, S., Means, R. and Leather, P. (1990) *Housing in Later Life: The Housing Finance Implications of an Ageing Society.* Bristol: School of Advanced Urban Studies.

Marshall, M. (1993) *Small Scale, Domestic Style, Longstay Accommodation for People with Dementia.* Dementia Services Development Centre, University of Stirling.

McCafferty, P. (1994) *Living Independently: A Study of the Housing Needs of Elderly and Disabled People.* London: HMSO.

McGlone, F. (1992) *Disability and Dependency: A Demographic and Moral Audit,* Occasional Paper 14. London: Family Policy Studies Centre.

McGlone, F. (1993) A million more carers – but how many more to come? In *Family Policy Bulletin,* June. London: Family Policy Studies Centre.

Meacher, M. (1972) *Taken for a Ride: Special Residential Homes for Confused Old People.* London: Longman.

Means, R. (1991) Community care, housing and older people: continuity or change? *Housing Studies,* 6(4): 273–84.

Means, R. and Smith, R. (1985) *The Development of Welfare Services for Elderly People.* London: Croom Helm.

Middleton, L. (1987) *So Much for So Few: A View of Sheltered Housing,* Occasional Papers 3. Institute of Human Ageing, University of Liverpool.

Ministry of Health (1949) *Report of the Ministry of Health for the year end 31 March 1948,* Cmd. 7734. London: HMSO.

Ministry of Health (1950) *Report of the Ministry of Health for the year end 31 March 1949,* Cmd. 7910. London: HMSO.

Ministry of Health (1955) *Report of the Ministry of Health for the year end 31 March 1954,* Cmd. 9566. London: HMSO.

Ministry of Health (1956) *Report of the Ministry of Health for the year end 31 March for1955,* Cmd. 9857. London: HMSO.

Ministry of Health (1962) *Local Authority Building Note No. 2. Residential Accommodation for Elderly People.* London: HMSO.

Ministry of Housing and Local Government (1969) *Housing Standards and Costs: Accommodation Specially Designed for Old People,* Circular 82/69. London: HMSO.

Morris, J. (1991) *Pride against Prejudice: Transforming Attitudes to Disability.* London: The Women's Press.

Morris, J. (1995) Creating a space for absent voices: disabled women's experiences of receiving assistance with daily living activities. *Feminist Review,* 51 (Autumn): 68–93.

Murphy, E. and MacDonald, A. (1994) The origins of the Project: The Domus philosophy. In E. Murphy, J. Lindesay and R. Dean (eds), *The Domus Project.* London: The Sainsbury Centre for Mental Health.

Murphy, E., Lindesay, J. and Dean, R. (eds) (1994) *The Domus Project: Long-term Care for Older People with Dementia.* London: The Sainsbury Centre for Mental Health.

National Association of Health Authorities [and Trusts] (1985) *Registration and inspection of Nursing Homes: A Handbook for Health Authorities.* Birmingham: NAHA.

National Association of Health Authorities and Trusts (1988) *Registration and Inspection of Nursing Homes: A Handbook for Health Authorities – Supplement.* Birmingham: NAHAT.

National Federation of Housing Associations (1987) *A Guide to the Registered Homes Act.* London: NFHA.

National Federation of Housing Associations (1993) *Pensioners Face Worse Affordability Problems.* London: NFHA.

National Institute for Social Work (1988a) *Residential Care: A Positive Choice.* London: HMSO.

National Institute for Social Work (1988b) *Residential Care: The Research Reviewed.* London: HMSO.

National Institute for Social Work (1990) *Staffing in Residential Care Homes,* Wagner Development Group. London: NISW.

National Institute for Social Work (1993) *Residential Care: Positive Answers.* London: HMSO.

Neill, J., Sinclair, I., Gorbach, P. and Williams, J. (1988) *A Need for Care? Elderly Applicants for Local Authority Homes.* Aldershot: Avebury.

Netten, A. (1992) Assessing the effect of social environment on demented elderly people in residential care. In K. Morgan (ed.), *Gerontology: Responding to An Ageing Society.* London: Jessica Kingsley.

Nissel, M. and Bonnerjea, L. (1982) *Family Care of the Elderly: Who Pays?* London: Policy Studies Institute.

Norman, A. (1980) *Rights and Risks.* London: Centre for Policy on Ageing.

Norman, A. (1985) *Triple Jeopardy: Growing Old in a Second Homeland.* Policy Studies in Ageing No. 3. London: Centre for Policy on Ageing.

Nuffield Foundation (1947) *Old People. Report of a Survey Committee on the Problems of Ageing and the Care of Old People, under the Chairmanship of B. Seebohm Rowntree.* London: Oxford University Press.

Office of Population Censuses and Surveys (1996) *Social Trends No. 26.* London: HMSO.

Office of Population Censuses and Surveys and General Register Office for Scotland (1993) *1991 Census. Persons Aged 60 and Over. Great Britain.* London: HMSO.

O'Kell, S. (1995) *Care Standards in the Residential Care Sector.* YPS for the Joseph Rowntree Foundation. York: York Publishing Services Ltd.

Oldman, C (1990) *Moving in Old Age: New Directions in Housing Policies.* London: HMSO.

Opit, L. and Pahl, J. (1993) Institutional care for elderly people: can we predict admissions. *Research, Policy and Planning,* 10(2): 2–5.

Parker, G. and Lawton, D. (1990a) *Further Analysis of the 1985 General Household Survey Data on Informal Care. Report I. A Typology of Caring.* Social Policy Research Unit, University of York,

Parker, G. and Lawton, D. (1990b) *Further Analysis of the 1985 General Household Survey Data on Informal Care Report 2: The Consequences of Caring.* Social Policy Research Unit, University of York.

Parker, R.A. (1981) Tending and social policy. In E.M. Goldberg and S. Hatch (eds), *A New Look at the Personal Social Services.* London: Policy Studies Institute.

Patel, N. (1990) *A 'Race' against Time? Social Services Provision to Black Elders.* London: Runnymede Trust.

Payne, C. (1994) *Evaluating the Quality of Care: A Self-assessment Manual.* London: NISW.

Peace, S.M. (1986) The design of residential homes: an historical perspective. In K. Judge and I. Sinclair (eds), *Residential Care for Elderly People.* London: HMSO.

Peace, S.M. (1987) Residential accommodation for dependent elderly people in Britain: the relationship between spatial structure and individual lifestyle. *Éspace, Populations, Sociétiés,* 1: 281–90.

Peace, S.M. (1988) Living environments for the elderly 2: Promoting the 'right' institutional environment. In N. Wells and C. Freer (eds), *The Ageing Population: Burden or Challenge?* London: Macmillan Press, 217–34.

Peace, S.M. (1993a) Quality of institutional life. *Reviews in Clinical Gerontology,* 3: 187–93.

Peace, S.M. (1993b) The living environments of older women. In M. Bernard and K. Meade (eds), *Women Come of Age.* London: Edward Arnold.

Peace, S.M. and Holland, C.A. (1994) Gender, ageing and our understanding of home: a review of underlying influences. Paper presented at the Gender and Ageing Conference, University of Surrey, July.

Peace, S.M., Kellaher, L. and Willcocks, D. (1982) *A Balanced Life? A Consumer Study of Residential Life in 100 Local Authority Old People's Homes,* Research report No. 14, Social Research Unit, Polytechnic of North London.

Personal Social Services Council (1977) *Residential Care Reviewed: Report of the Residential Care Working Party.* London: PSSC.

Pfeffer, N. and Coote, A. (1991) *Is Quality Good for You? A Critical Review of Quality Assurance in Welfare Services.* London: Institute for Public Policy Research.

Phillips, J. (1992) *Private Residential Care: The Admission Process and Reactions of the Public Sector.* Aldershot: Avebury.

Phillipson, C. and Biggs, S. (1992) *Understanding Elder Abuse: A Training Manual for the Helping Professions.* London: Longman.

Pitkeathley, J. (1991) The carers' viewpoint. In G. Dalley (ed.) *Disability and Social Policy.* London: Policy Studies Institute, 203–4.

Policy Studies Institute (1993) *Newssheet. Caring for People Who Live at Home,* Issue No. 1 (Autumn). London: PSI.

Qureshi, H. and Walker, A. (1989) *The Caring Relationship: Elderly People and Their Families.* London: Macmillan.

Reed, J. and Roskell Payton, V. (1995a) Accomplishing friendships in nursing and residential homes. Paper presented at the Third European Congress of Gerontology, Amsterdam, September.

Reed, J. and Roskell Payton, V. (1995b) Settling in and moving on: the transition to care homes. Paper presented at the British Society of Gerontology Annual Conference, University of Keele, September.

Residential Forum (1996) *Creating a Home from Home: A Guide to Standards.* London: NISW.

Robb, B. (ed.) (1967) *Sans Everything: A Case to Answer.* London: Nelson.

Rolfe, S., Leather, P. and Mackintosh, S. (1993) *Available Options: The Constraints Facing Older People in Meeting Housing and Care Needs.* Oxford: Anchor Housing Trust.

Roose, T. (1996) Lessons for a sheltered past. *Voluntary Housing,* March: 6–7.

Rosser, C. and Harris, C. (1965) *The Family in Social Change.* London: Routledge and Kegan Paul.

Rowntree, B. Seebohm (1910) *Poverty: A Study of Town Life.* London: Macmillan.

Royal College of Nursing (1992) *A Scandal Waiting to Happen.* London: RCN.

Royal Commission on Poor Laws and Relief of Distress (1909) *Report,* Cmd. 4499. London: HMSO.

Rubenstein, R.L. and Parmelee, P.A. (1992) Attachment to place and the representation of the life course by the elderly. In I. Altman and S.M. Low (eds), *Place Attachment.* New York: Plenum Press.

Saunders, P. (1990) *A Nation of Inheritors.* London: Unwin Hyman.

Savishinsky, J. (1991) *The Ends of Time: Life and Work in a Nursing Home.* New York: Bergen and Garvey.

Schneider, J., Mann, A., Mozley, C., Abbey, A., Netten, A., Topan, C. and Levin, E. (1996) *An Exploration of the Measures of Quality of Care: Final Report of a Study funded through Northern and Yorkshire NHS Executive.* London: Institute of Psychiatry, NISW and PPSEU.

Sealy, A. (1995) Housing with care. *Access by Design,* 67 (May/August): 10–13.

Sinclair, I. (1988) The elderly. In NISW, *The Research Reviewed.* London: HMSO.

Sinclair, I. (1990) Residential care. In I. Sinclair, R. Parker, D. Leat and J. Williams (eds), *The Kaleidoscope of Care.* London: HMSO.

Sinclair, I. and Williams, J. (1990) Setting-based services. In I. Sinclair, R. Parker, D. Leat and J. Williams (eds), *The Kaleidoscope of Care.* London: HMSO.

Sinclair, I., Parker, R., Leat, D. and Williams, J. (eds) (1990) *The Kaleidoscope of Care: A Review of Research on Welfare Provision for Elderly People*. London: HMSO.

Sixsmith, J. and Sixsmith, A. (1990) Places in transition: the impact of life events on the experience of home. In T. Putnam and C. Newton (eds), *Household Choice*. London: Futura.

Smith, C. (1992) The geography of private residential care. In K. Morgan (ed.), *Gerontology: Responding to An Ageing Society*. London: Jessica Kingsley, 99–117.

Smith, H. and Brown, H. (1992) Defending community care: can normalization do the job? *British Journal of Social Work*, 22(6): 685–93.

Social Policy Research Unit (1987) Private residential care and public funds. *Cash & Care. The Newsletter of the SPRU*, 2 (Autumn).

Szasz, T.S. (1961) *The Myth of Mental Illness: Foundations of a Theory of Personal Conduct*. New York: Dell.

Szivos, S. (1992) The limits of integration? In H. Brown and H. Smith (eds), *Normalisation: a Reader for the 90's*. London: Routledge.

Thompson, P., Itzin, C. and Abendstern, M. (1990) *I Don't Feel Old: Understanding the Experience of Later Life*. Oxford: Oxford University Press.

Thorns, D.C. (1994) The role of housing inheritance in selected owner-occupied societies. *Housing Studies*, 9(4): 473–510.

Tinker, A. (1989) *An Evaluation of Very Sheltered Housing*. London: HMSO.

Titmuss, R.M. (1963) *Essays on 'the Welfare State'*, 2nd edn. London: Allen & Unwin.

Tobin, S.S. (1989) The effects of institutionalisation. In K.S. Markides and C.L. Cooper (eds), *Aging, Stress and Health*. New York: Wiley.

Tobin, S.S. and Lieberman, M.A. (1976) *Last Home for the Aged: Critical Implications of Institutionalization*. San Francisco: Jossey-Bass.

Townsend, P. (1957) *The Family Life of Old People*. London: Routledge.

Townsend, P. (1962) *The Last Refuge*. London: Routledge and Kegan Paul.

Townsend, P. (1972) The needs of the elderly and planning of hospitals. In R.W. Canvin and N.G. Pearson (eds), *Needs of the Elderly for Health and Welfare Services*. University of Exeter Press.

Townsend, P. (1981) The structured dependency of the elderly: the creation of social policy in the twentieth century. *Ageing and Society*, 1(1): 5–28.

Townsend, P. (1986) Ageism and social policy. In C. Phillipson and A. Walker (eds), *Ageing and Social Policy*. London: Gower.

Twigg, J., Atkins, K. and Perring, C. (1990) *Carers and Services: A Review of the Research*. London: HMSO.

Wade, B., Sawyer, L. and Bell, J. (1983) *Dependency with Dignity*, Occasional Papers in Social Administration No.68. London: Bedford Square Press.

Wagner Development Group (1990) *Staffing in Residential Care Homes*. London: NISW.

Wagner Development Group (1993) *Security of tenure in Residential Homes: Code for a Contract*. London: NISW.

Walker, A. (1993) Poverty and inequality in old age. In J. Bond, P. Coleman and S. Peace (eds), *Ageing in Society: An Introduction to Social Gerontology*, 2nd edn. London: Sage.

Wardhaugh, T. and Wilding, P. (1993) Towards an explanation of the corruption of care. *Critical Social Policy*, 37: 4–31.

Watson, L. and Cooper, R. (1992) *Housing with Care: Supported Housing and Housing Associations*. York: Joseph Rowntree Foundation.

Weaver, T., Willcocks, D. and Kellaher, L. (1985) *The Business of Care: A Study of Private Residential Homes for Old People*. CESSA, London: Polytechnic of North London.

Webb, S. and Webb, B. (1910) *English Poor Law Policy*. London: Longmans, Green and Co.

Webb, S. and Webb, B. (1927) *English Poor Law Policy, Part 1: The Old Poor Law*. London: Longmans, Green and Co.

White, D. (1994) *On Being the Relative of Someone in a Home*. London: The Relatives Association.

Wilkin, D. and Hughes, B. (1987) Residential care of elderly people: the consumers' views. *Ageing and Society,* 7(2): 175–202.

Wilkin, D. and Jolley, D. (1979) *Behavioural Problems among Old People in Geriatric Wards: Psychogeriatric Wards and Residential Homes 1976–78,* Research report No. 1, Psychogeriatric Unit, University of South Manchester.

Willcocks, D., Peace, S., Kellaher, L. with Ring, A. (1982) *The Residential Life of Old People: A Study of 100 Local Authority Old People's Homes,* Vol. 1. Research report No. 12, Survey Research Unit, Polytechnic of North London.

Willcocks, D., Peace, S. and Kellaher, L. (1987) *Private Lives in Public Places*. London: Tavistock Publications.

Williams, S. and Dickins, A. (1994) Key steps towards a domiciliary care contract. *Community Care Management and Planning,* 2(3): 83–91.

Willmott, P. and Young, M. (1957) *Family and Kinship in East London*. London: Penguin Books.

Willmott, P. and Young, M. (1960) *Family and Class in a London Suburb,* London: Routledge and Kegan Paul.

Wistow, G. (1995) Aspirations and realities: community care at the crossroads. *Health and Social Care in the Community,* 3(4): 227–40.

Wolfensberger, W. (1972) *The Principle of Normalization in Human Services*. Toronto: National Institute on Mental Retardation.

Wolfensberger, W. (1995) Social role valorization is too conservative. No, it is too radical. *Disability and Society,* 10(3): 365–7.

Women's Design Service (1991) *Designing Housing for Older Women*. London: Women's Design Service.

Woodward, K. (1991) *Aging and Its Discontents: Freud and Other Fictions*. Bloomington and Indianapolis: Indiana University Press.

Youll, P.J. and McCourt-Perring, C. (1993) *Raising Voices: Ensuring Quality in Residential Care*. London: HMSO.

Index